OPENING HEAVEN'S DOORS

A Scriptural Guide to Carrying Out God's Plan of Salvation

> We loved you so much that we were delighted to share
> with you not only the gospel of God but our lives as well,
> because you had become so dear to us.
> **1Thessalonians 2:8**
> DeColores!
> Mike & Roxy Lynch

by
Dr. Paul L. Engstrom, Th.D.

WINNING PUBLICATIONS
2372 Leibel St.
White Bear Lake, MN 55110

First Edition: May, 1997

Printed in the United States of America

ISBN: 1-884367-02-X

Dedication

To Lynn
A companion whose qualities exceed her purview, whose gifts sustain and inspire in ever-increasing measure.

Also to Rachel and Jennifer
The wonder and joy they provide continually surpass comprehension.

Acknowledgements

My brother, David M. Engstrom and good friend, Daniel J. Pilla, have provided the acumen and support necessary to bring this project to its present form. Their contributions, which encompass more than mundane things, will not be forgotten.

Table of Contents

About the Author . . .

Paul L. Engstrom has a rich and varied academic background, earning his Doctor of Theology degree at Luther Theological Seminary in St. Paul, Minnesota in 1996. Spending five years in this program, his interests lay primarily in the Pentateuch and poetic literature of the Old Testament. Dr. Engstrom also developed expertise with representative poetic literature of the larger ancient Near Eastern environment, primarily that of Canaan and Babylon.

Prior to his doctorate work, he earned a Master of Arts in Theology degree in 1988 at Bethel Theological Seminary, also in St. Paul. His program concentrations were Hebrew, Greek and general Bible. In 1982, he earned his Bachelor of Science degree in pastoral studies.

As a college professor, Dr. Engstrom instructed students in Old and New Testament Bible courses and also New Testament Greek. He held a pastoral staff position for nine years and was a senior pastor for five more. Having had both academic and practical experience, Dr. Engstrom is uniquely qualified to expound on Scriptures in a way relevant to the needs of today's Christians. His book, *Opening Heaven's Doors* is the culmination of a lifetime of effort and experience, presenting a fresh and challenging exploration into both the Bible and contemporary Christian life.

Therefore, brethren, be the more zealous to confirm your call and election, for if you do this you will never fall; so there will be richly provided for you an entrance into the eternal kingdom of our Lord and Savior Jesus Christ (2 Pet 1:10-11).

Introduction

Opening Heaven's Doors is written for those who are serious about their Christianity, hoping one day to reap the eternal reward awaiting those who diligently seek it. The message contained is decidedly not for those who are looking for easy access into the eternal kingdom, because such access does not exist.

The simple truth derived from the biblical literature is that much human effort must accompany the gracious act of Jesus Christ on the cross of Calvary. Christians are absolutely required to put into practice what they have received by God's grace. The gracious act is not enough; if it was, there would be no need for scriptural instruction.

Divided into five chapters, *Opening Heaven's Doors* is biblically-based, meaning two things: (1) it is fiercely devoted to the truth of Scripture rather than the whims and philosophical musings of humanity, and (2) it utilizes extensively both testaments, not presuming one to be any more or less inspired than the other.

The first chapter delineates the mandate concerning participation in the community, how the bearing of fruit is absolutely essential for any person claiming an association with

God. If the lives of others are not positively affected by a so-called "Christian's" life, then that person's habits and attitudes are in need of immediate re-examination.

The process of salvation is never claimed to be an easy one. Using Jeremiah as an example, it is argued that perseverance and diligence are in no way optional for the God-fearing believer; without them, a person stands little or no chance of attaining a state of final salvation.

Chapter two speaks of the inner change that must occur in the life of a believer; without a transformation of the heart and soul, the outer workings of righteousness are not forthcoming, and consequently, God's expectations are not met. In addition to a discussion concerning the former sinful nature, there is instruction related to attitudes, dispositions and temperament. Clearly, a person must be inwardly renewed and transformed if that person's life is to mean anything to the community at large.

The third chapter moves into an examination of what constitutes an appropriate manifestation of the Christian life, always keeping in the mind that the outward signs of "righteousness" must be in harmony with the inward renewal process. What is re-emphasized is the importance of the community and how the Christian person must always have a positive effect, not only on the larger body of believers, but the non-believers as well.

Once a person has found true inward renewal and is practicing a lifestyle paralleling that renewal, a state of being must be born that is regular and consistent. Chapter four discusses this settled approach to life that constrains a person to be humble and obedient, serving both God and humanity without regard for self.

Also contained is a self diagnostic test of sorts derived from the book of James. It enables a person to examine himself by gauging the extent to which he has conformed to the biblical principles expounded in this book. Not the least of these indicators is the use of the tongue. Additional time is spent on this issue for two reasons: (1) the Bible itself considers this topic important enough to make repeated reference to it, and (2) the way in which the tongue is used is an extremely accurate measurement of a person's progress in the faith.

The final chapter offers six practical applications of the four chapters which precede it. For most people, it is helpful to receive direct counsel as to what is expected of them as Christians. This chapter provides some inexhaustive assistance in this area.

Determinations regarding "righteousness" and a person's salvation or lack thereof, must be left to the individual. It is not possible for another to judge, for there is no way of reasonably discerning all that lies behind a person's actions and attitudes; perceptions are inescapably based on incomplete information and unavoidable presuppositions.

The guidance in this book is meant to be just that: guidance; it is, very simply, an attempt to expound on scriptural principles which are both certain and conspicuous. It is the firm conviction of this author that the person attempting diligently to accomplish what lies in these five chapters will be doing well and will, one day, see the doors of heaven open.

The wall was built of jasper, while the city was pure gold, clear as glass. The foundations of the wall of the city were adorned with every jewel; the first was jasper, the second sapphire, the third agate, the fourth emerald, the fifth onyx, the sixth carnelian, the seventh chrysolite, the eighth beryl, the ninth topaz, the tenth chrysoprase, the eleventh jacinth, the twelfth amethyst. And the twelve gates were twelve pearls, each of the gates made of a single pearl, and the street of the city was pure gold, transparent as glass (Rev 21:18-21).

CHAPTER ONE
Making Heaven Your Destination

The Mandate Concerning Community

Few things emerge from God's Word with greater clarity than that concerning the primacy of relationships. Scriptural teaching makes preposterous the notion that Christianity exists in isolation from a relationship with God. What is equally inconceivable is the notion that a relationship with God exists apart from the relationships we develop and sustain with one another. The book of Micah provides illumination.

In the sixth chapter, a court case of cosmic proportions is being tried. God is prosecutor, the nation Israel is defendant, and the very foundations of the earth have been called to serve as jury. With the three primary components of creation in attendance, this is clearly no small matter.

Hear what the LORD says: Arise, plead your case before the mountains, and let the hills hear your voice.   Hear, you mountains, the controversy of the LORD, and you enduring foundations of the earth; for the LORD has a controversy with his people, and he will contend with Israel (Mic 6:1-2).

The cosmic atmosphere is indicative of the epidemic proportions of Israel's sins, but it also suggests the paradigmatic nature of the forthcoming denunciation; it speaks to the nation Israel, but it speaks also to the people of God in all generations.

O my people, what have I done to you? In what have I wearied you? Answer me! For I brought you up from the land of Egypt, and redeemed you from the house of bondage; and I sent before you Moses, Aaron, and Miriam. O my people, remember what Balak king of Moab devised, and what Balaam the son of Be'or answered him, and what happened from Shittim to Gilgal, that you may know the saving acts of the LORD (Mic 6:3-5).

The point is that God's people have been deprived of nothing. Divine provision secured for the Israelites (1) deliverance from the Egyptians, (2) leaders who offered guidance, (3) protection from enemies, and (4) entrance into the Promised Land.

As God recounts His activity on behalf of His people, the progression noted is nothing if not familiar to contemporary Christians: (1) redemption is granted, (2) support is offered, and (3) promises are fulfilled. Unfortunately, what is also familiar is the response (or the lack thereof) of the nation Israel to the divine effort. There is no devotion, no sense of duty or obligation, and no apparent desire to offer any kind of repayment.

It is not surprising, that as God indicts an entire nation for their wrongdoing, the initial reaction is one of silence. No explanations are forthcoming because there are none appropriate. No excuses are offered because there are none acceptable.

After an indeterminate amount of time, the silence is broken when a single voice rises from the midst of the assembly. Apparently, there is but one person among the thousands who feels compelled to make an attempt at restitution.

> With what shall I come before the LORD, and bow myself before God on high? Shall I come before him with burnt offerings, with calves a year old? Will the LORD be pleased with thousands of rams, with ten thousands of rivers of oil? Shall I give my first-born for my transgression, the fruit of my body for the sin of my soul? (Mic 6:7-8)

In one sense, the lengths to which this individual is willing to go is admirable. His suggestions for payment begin with something comparatively small, and progress to that which he values above all else. Clearly, the message he offers is a willingness to do absolutely anything.

But, in another sense, we cannot help but be discouraged. For the person who possesses the most commendable qualities among all the people of God, the one for whom we hold out the most hope, is found to be woefully lacking in His understanding of God, and God's expectations of His people. There is a desire to make restitution, but there is also in evidence nothing short of a gross misunderstanding of God Himself.

He has showed you, O man, what is good; and what does the LORD require of you but to do justice, and to love kindness, and to walk humbly with your God? (Mic 6:8)

These words make clear the individual's misconception concerning restitution, for God is not interested in the various options presented. He is not interested in the offerings of rams, and oil, and first-born children. God's expectations have nothing to do with what He can receive from His people. On the contrary, the divine conception of restitution has to do with the treatment His people offer one another.

Clearly, God does not require conciliation for Himself. He has no desire to receive some "thing," some meaningless display that is easily offered with an obligatory air, devoid of sincerity. God demands that which is far more meaningful, for God demands that which is the essence of who His people are.

In summary, God is responsible for His people receiving (1) deliverance, (2) support, and (3) fulfilled promises. In return, God asks His people to devote themselves, to *one another* with the utmost integrity. The prescription is somewhat remarkable when we consider that it was God who was dealt the various injustices, yet God's answer to the question related to recompense has to do with God's people (1) doing justice, (2) loving kindness, and (3) walking humbly with Him.

"Do Justice"

To "do justice" has to do with the practice of who we are in the everyday sphere of life. To "do justice" can easily be translated, "act justly," and is therefore concerned with the decisions we make as we interact with one another. It does not mean we justify our actions simply because they are legally or politically correct. In fact, concepts such as these are meant to be transcended as we relate to one another in ways which reflect an appreciation of what God has done for us. To conduct ourselves otherwise is to express a dissatisfaction with what we have received from God, specifically, His redemption, support and faithfulness.

This is certainly one of the main points of the story we find in Matthew 18. In this parable, the kingdom of heaven is compared to a king who wished to settle accounts with his servants. One particular servant was unable to pay, and instead of exercising his right to sell the man and his family, the king released the servant from his debt.

Interestingly enough, that same servant came upon a man who owed him a sum of money which could not be paid. And instead of dispensing mercy, the servant chose to exercise his legal right to have the man thrown into jail. When the king heard this, he summoned his servant before him, labeled him as wicked, reinstated the debt previously forgiven, and had him thrown into prison.

The king rightly interpreted the servant's actions as reflective of a profound lack of appreciation for what was received. Although the servant was perfectly willing to accept unmerited favor offered him, there remained an unwillingness to dispense the same to others. This prompted the only reasonable conclusion; that which was received was done so on only the most superficial of levels.

This story is recorded in the hope that self-examination might issue forth transformation. And such profound results would be good. But there is also contained within this story a disturbing truth related to the inherent self-centeredness that occupies much of society, even Christian society today. This pre-occupation with self is, at the very least, an eroding force; at its worst, it is that which obliterates any hope of reproducing the character of God in this world. And when this happens, there is failure of insurmountable proportions.

As the instruction to, "do justice" comes, there is much more than simple guidance being offered the nation of Israel. There is more than a hasty suggestion being offered to treat some insignificant problem. Much more than these, there is instruction, which, if practiced, is that which is reflective of God Himself. We must not accept these words as perfunctory rhetoric, but that which is directly expressive of the divine presence. "Practice justice."

"Love Kindness"

The second prescription offered the remorseful individual is simply, "love kindness." Like the first prescription, if this one is to be followed, it must necessarily be practiced. And naturally, it can be practiced only in the company of others, never in isolation.

From this passage, it is clear that "kindness" (also translated as "goodness," "lovingkindness" and "steadfast love") is something to be practiced by humanity. But for the term and its accompanying practice to be understood, it is perhaps best to see how the same term is used in relation to God.

First of all, many scriptural portions refer to the "kindness" of God as being that which is abundant. (e.g. Exod 34:6; Ps 103:8; Jonah 4:2). For example, when the "glory" of the LORD passed by Moses in Exodus 34, God's self-proclamation was, "The LORD, the LORD, a God merciful and gracious, slow to anger and abounding in *steadfast love* and faithfulness" (Exod 34:6). These words become more significant when we are reminded that they come shortly after the incident with the golden calf (Exod 32), when the Lord was so angry, he expressed to Moses His desire to destroy the people (Exod 32:10).

The Hebrew word from which "kindness" is translated (hesed) has a meaning which is difficult to comprehend by way of wordy definitions. The essential nature of hesed begins to become clear to us as we reflect upon its abundant provision in the midst of circumstances which are anything but favorable for such a display. To grasp God's self-proclaimed "steadfast love" ("kindness") in Exodus 34, for example, we need to first build context, backing up to Exodus 32.

In Exodus 32, God's people are at their worst as they exhibit a blatant disregard for all of God's previous efforts on their behalf. At the base of Mount Sinai, the Israelites respond to their new-found liberation by making an offering. Naturally, one would expect this offering to be directed toward God. But instead, it is directed toward that which God opposes.

The gold which made up this offering was not requested of the people, as it was for the building of God's tabernacle in Exodus 35. Instead, the people receive a command to give up their gold (Exod 32:2). And when Aaron received it, he "fashioned it with a graving tool, and made a molten calf" (Exod 32:4). On the next morning, the people rose early "and offered burnt offerings and brought peace offerings; and the people sat down to eat and drink, and rose up to play" (Exod 32:6).

Amazingly, the people respond to God's efforts by giving honor to another; they respond to their God-given salvation by constructing and subsequently worshipping a golden calf. That the Israelites' behavior was beneath contempt is not in question, but before we cast the proverbial stone, let us remind ourselves that the Israelites exhibit that which is, once again, all too familiar to us. The sad truth is that the vast majority of those who today condemn the Israelites, simultaneously bring condemnation upon themselves.

Whatever it was that caused the Israelites to ignore that which was so graciously provided, is still a force to be reckoned with today. People often times express precisely the opposite of what is deserved. And even though it sounds preposterous, and truly is, these absurdities are practiced with great regularity. As a result, relationships with God suffer terribly, and relationships within the community of faith never even come close to realizing what are the expectations of God.

What is within human nature that is the cause of behavior that produces such devastating effects? Is it fear of commitment? Is it a stubborn refusal to become subordinate? Is it an inability to give something other than that which is self-gratifying? Unfortunately, all three, in some measure, can probably be used to weigh what is the substance of humankind.

Exodus 32 demonstrates at least two disturbing realities. First of all, people have a tendency to respond to the gracious acts of God in ways which are wholly inappropriate. God puts forth great effort on behalf of His people, and all too often, they respond with demonstrations of disloyalty and self-service. Before the molten calf, there is clearly the presence of ingratitude. But beyond this, a display of such proportions indicates an aversion to who God is, and what are His intentions. Exodus 32 demonstrates nothing if not resistance to God and His purpose.

Secondly, people are predisposed to self-gratification and consequently, their involvement with one another speaks to the most superficial of levels. When the people "sat down to eat and drink, and rose up to play" (Exod 32:6), there is painted a clear portrait of carnality. However, this portrait speaks to more than this, for the "sitting down" and "rising up" points to that which goes beyond a momentary act; it points to that which reflects a procedure of life. Sadly, it points to people who have devoted themselves to the same people for whom they show exclusive concern: themselves. The relationships which result do not find divine sanction. In fact, they are relationships constitutive of all God opposes, and of all God "does not require" of His people.

If we view Exodus 32 as a study in human nature, it is unsettling, to say the least. It is, among other things, an uncomfortable reminder of our own inadequacies when it comes to relationships. Concerning our relationship with God and those relationships we share with each other, there is a tendency to be both selfish and near-sighted. And when we live between egocentrism and myopia, our first thought is, inescapably, for ourselves.

When our vision cannot extend beyond our own wants and needs, it is impossible to relate to God and to His people in a manner that God "requires." With this visual limitation, it is an effort in futility to discern what are the wants and needs of others, for we cannot even see to the limits of our own.

As disturbing as this scene is at the base of Mount Sinai in Exodus 32, ironically, it assists in the comprehension of God's self-proclamation of "kindness" expressed in Exodus 34. When "kindness" is God's response to such rejection, debauchery, and insolence, we begin to understand just how abundant the "kindness" of God really is. It is the degree to which God was "kind" toward the Israelites in Exodus 34 that we are expected to be kind to one another.

According to Micah 6, there is an appropriate response to all that God has done for His people, specifically, to God's (1) deliverance, (2) support, and (3) fulfilled promises. And this response has much to do with the way God's people associate, not with God, but with one another. They are to "do justice," and "love kindness." But there is a third prescription given by Micah, and that is "to walk humbly with your God."

"Walk Humbly With Your God"

If a person were told the first two prescriptions ("do justice," and "love kindness") were answers to a question, and was then asked to suggest what the question might be, chances are the person's suggestion would have nothing to do with an inquiry concerning how a sinful person might offer restitution to God. People, very simply, do not typically think in terms reflective of such unselfishness. They do not "walk humbly" with God or with each other.

It is sad commentary, but what is much more reasonable to many people is the idea of intentionally fostering feelings of indebtedness, withholding forgiveness that transgressions committed against them might be used to their own advantage. People such as these are like the Israelites before the golden calf, deriving from whatever circumstances are before them whatever personal benefit is available.

Fortunately, God does not operate in this manner. In the book of Exodus, for example, the salvation of the Israelites was secured without any pre-existing requirements. God did not first ask what the people would give in exchange for their deliverance. It was only after the Israelites were redeemed from the hands of their oppressors that God offered them His terms for a covenant relationship. Speaking to Moses on Sinai, God says,

> Thus you shall say to the house of Jacob, and tell the people of Israel: You have seen what I did to the Egyptians, and how I bore you on eagles' wings and brought you to myself. Now therefore, if you will obey my voice and keep my covenant, you shall be my own possession among all peoples; for all the earth is mine, and you shall be to me a kingdom of priests and a holy nation (Exod 19:4-6).

It is important to observe that no demands are made of the people. With salvation already in their grasp, they were allowed to either accept or reject God's terms. Clearly, the relationship God had in mind was one based upon mutual agreement.

In these latter days, God's salvation has appeared in a similar fashion. As God "came down to deliver" (Exod 3:8) the Israelites, so has Jesus Christ descended into the world. He came without first proposing terms, or establishing guidelines. Through Him, salvation has been offered freely, and any person willing to accept that salvation may do so.

Jesus Christ is the most poignant expression of God's desire to cover sin, and forget transgression. Through God's Son, iniquities are not wielded as a weapon against God's people, that God's people might submit to His authority. Iniquities are simply and decidedly covered.

In Micah 6, the penitent man steps forward and asks how he might provide restitution for sins committed. In response, God tells him to "do justice" and "love kindness," prescriptions which, on the surface, may seem to have nothing to do with a sin offering to God. At first, it may seem as though the inquiry was miscommunicated in some way, but the third prescription is then offered: "Walk humbly with your God." When it is, there remains no question that the first two prescriptions were indeed spoken in response to the question put forth.

Love Your Neighbor

The three prescriptions of Micah 6, taken together, accomplish what no other single verse of Scripture is able to accomplish. They provide what is the heart and substance of a scriptural definition of a relationship with God by linking ethics with godliness, and duty toward God with duty toward humankind. Jesus teaches the same when asked what is the greatest commandment.

> And he said to him, "You shall love the Lord your God with all your heart, and with all your soul, and with all your mind. This is the great and first commandment. And a second is like it, You shall love your neighbor as yourself. On these two commandments depend all the law and the prophets (Matt 22:37-40).

The passages in Micah and Matthew make clear that religion involves more than the fulfillment of obligations to God. An inner experience is involved, but religion must also determine the entire sphere of human existence. It must determine actions, but more than this, it must circumscribe character.

In Micah 6, the man who stepped forward was clearly misinformed concerning his obligations to God. The various options he related regarding recompense all concerned certain sacrifices which could be made. But, more than this, these options involved activity which would be accomplished in isolation. And God would not hear of it.

It is true that God is not necessarily pleased with external activities, for physical operation does not necessarily project anything even closely resembling truth or substance. In fact, it can be a powerful tool of deception. But the man in Micah 6 was plainly not staging his remorse, for he was willing to give up his wealth, and even his son.

God was still displeased with the man's suggestions, but not because He believed the man was insincere, or attempting to "sacrifice away" his guilt. Primarily, God's comments were directed toward the man's lack of commitment to the larger body of believers. This lack of commitment is apparent in the man's proposals for restitution, for these proposals have nothing to do with the community.

This lack of regard for the community of faith almost certainly affected all members of Israel. Furthermore, there is little question that such self-centeredness traveled a course parallel to that of Israel's deteriorating relationship with God, and therefore, was the primary reason God called the people before Him in the first place.

As Israel is gathered before God, it becomes obvious that the people's relationship with God is not what it should be. But the instructions of God concerning restitution have to do with mending the relationships the people have with one another. He tells them to "do justice," and to "love kindness," making it clear that restitution is made when His people relate to one another in a way that is reflective of the way God relates to them.

Although these instructions were given to a man seeking atonement for his sins, we must not understand them to be applicable only when propitiation is being sought. Indeed, every person who associates with God is expected to, "love kindness" and "do justice" on a regular basis, making these a "settled" part of their daily procedure. With a certainty, these practices are reflection of the association itself and therefore, validate its authenticity.

That God has certain "communal expectations" of His people is illustrated in the New Testament as well. Words of Jesus recorded in Matthew 5 say,

> You have heard that it was said to the men of old, "You shall not kill; and whoever kills shall be liable to judgment." But I say to you that every one who is angry with his brother shall be liable to judgment; whoever insults his brother shall be liable to the council, and whoever says, "You fool!" shall be liable to the hell of fire. So if you are offering your gift at the altar, and there remember that your brother has something against you, leave your gift there before the altar and go; first be reconciled to your brother, and then come and offer your gift (Matt 5:21-24).

Like Micah, Matthew indicates that the offering of sacrifices are "less important" than relationships shared among God's people. Said another way, the relationships which are developed and sustained among God's people are to come before the relationship that is shared with God.

This can only mean that the two relationships run a parallel course, that they are both either intact or impaired. Jesus is not suggesting that earthly associations are more important than the spiritual one we share with God. But, at the same time, He does make clear their unalterable significance. Indeed, the association we have with God MUST manifest itself in the relationships we have with one another. If it does not, it is an offense to God.

These verses in Matthew 5 imply that unresolved earthly conflicts cause a person's relationship with God to be suspended. This is sobering as we reflect upon the many difficulties we have had with others, and the many difficulties that yet remain.

What is also sobering is the realization that Matthew 5 refers to the need for reconciliation, not when we have difficulty with a brother, but when a brother has difficulty with us. This is no small matter in that we have a tendency to absolve ourselves of responsibility when we are convinced we harbor no feelings of ill-will toward someone. According to Matthew, this is not good enough. We must also be convinced someone else is not harboring feelings of ill-will toward us. Only then are we free to progress in our relationship with God.

Bearing Fruit Is Not Optional

The first three verses of Psalm 1 illustrate so very well the high expectations, even demands of God regarding the relationships we have in this world. That it is the first psalm in the psalter is likely indicative of its importance in relation to the other psalms recorded.

Blessed is the man who walks not in the counsel of the wicked, nor stands in the way of sinners, nor sits in the seat of scoffers; but his delight is in the law of the LORD, and on his law he meditates day and night. He is like a tree planted by streams of water, that yields its fruit in its season, and its leaf does not wither. In all that he does, he prospers (Ps 1:1-3).

The word that stands at the entrance to the psalter is "blessed." It is a word that speaks of happiness and comfort experienced by those who "do" and "practice" in accordance with the expectations, indeed the mandates, of God. The word, "blessed" should always be seen as a signal to what is pleasing in the sight of the Lord.

In a way reminiscent of the beatitudes in Matthew 5, the psalmist praises the proper behavior of God's people. At the same time, he characterizes that behavior both negatively and positively in the first two verses.

In the first verse, the portrayal of that which is NOT pleasing to God is accomplished by the use of three phrases, all of which are progressively intensified. The first phrase is, "Blessed is the man who walks not in the counsel of the wicked." Simply said, those who allow themselves to be led by the advice of "evildoers" are in danger of becoming "evildoers" themselves.

Those people who are "wicked" or who can be categorized as "evildoers" are most appropriately understood as those who have little or no regard for God. Said another way, they are people whose intentions and plans and ambitions are neither born of God, or allowed to interact with God's will. "Evildoers" are self-willed and self-directed, making their counsel, at the very least, suspect. But more than this, those who seek out and receive such counsel are those who clearly prefer the advice of the "wicked" to the counsel of God. When this occurs, there is evidenced, once again, activity which is neither born of God or related to God's will.

The second phrase in verse 1 says a person will be "blessed" if that person "does not stand in the way of sinners." Although the first phrase also indicated sinful activity, the second phrase points to behavior which is one step further removed from God, therefore, more "wicked."

Here, there is more than inquiry into the ways of the wicked, and there is more than the entertainment of ideas spawned by the ungodly. In the second phrase, there is no longer a detached consideration of wickedness, but an active participation that is clearly intentional.

"Standing in the way of sinners" points to conformity. And as Hebrews 12 demonstrates, this is precisely the opposite of what God expects of His people.

> I appeal to you therefore, brethren, by the mercies of God, to present your bodies as a living sacrifice, holy and acceptable to God, which is your spiritual worship. Do not be conformed to this world but be transformed by the renewal of your mind, that you may prove what is the will of God, what is good and acceptable and perfect (Heb 12:1-2).

An association with "ungodly" people always places one in a position where the voice of God is heard less clearly than the voice of the "evildoers." And when people place themselves in this position, they leave themselves open to entering what is the psalmist's third and most serious state of being, that state where a person "sits in the seat of scoffers."

First of all, "scoffing" is done by those who are "settled" in their views. "Scoffing" comes from those who are so arrogant, so sure of their own ways and perspectives, that they feel justified in their derision and ridicule of others. And according to the psalmist, what God finds equally contemptible is the decision to identify oneself with such a group. And that is exactly what the person does who "sits in the seat of scoffers."

Verse one throws the conduct of God-fearing people into relief by three negative characterizations, all of which are progessively "more involved" in the lives of the "wicked." Identifying oneself with the wicked is more serious than being conformed to the wicked which is more serious than receiving counsel from the wicked.

Even though Psalm 1 contains the important reminder that sin has a tendency to build and become progressively "more complicating," we must remember that the psalmist considers all three activities to be sinful. All three most likely represent various dimensions of the sinful way of life, and clearly, not any one of the three dimensions is to be tolerated.

Again, it is made clear that earthly activity determines what is pleasing and displeasing to God. What we "do" and what we "practice" among other people, determines how acceptable or unacceptable is the relationship we have with God. The psalmist makes this plain in verse one as he negatively describes the activity of a person who is "blessed." This teaching is reiterated in verse two when the psalmist describes the activity of the same, but this time, in a positive manner.

The second verse defines the person with whom God is pleased as one whose delight "is in the law of the Lord, and on his law he meditates day and night." In this verse, God's law (instruction), which leads people in the correct way, is contrasted with the way of the "wicked ones" in verse one.

According to the psalmist, a person finds true happiness when God's will is practiced. And that the divine will is to be meditated upon unceasingly demonstrates a call for God's will to be more than superficial transposition of His laws which speak primarily to external behavior. Clearly, there is to be an internalization of God's will, that which speaks more to who we are rather than what we do.

Often times, God's laws are viewed as restrictive, nothing more than a list of do's and don'ts. Such a view does God's laws and God Himself a terrible disservice, for God's laws are not now, nor have they ever been some distant entity to be measured up to.

On the contrary, God's laws are personal and life-giving, meant to protect and support, not imprison and restrict. They testify of God's desire to be close to His people and offer them guidance for life. Those who understand this gladly meditate on God's laws to the point where God's will becomes second nature.

Both verses one and two of this psalm describe what makes a person "blessed" in the sight of God. Verse one does so by describing what a person should NOT do, and verse two by describing what a person SHOULD do. That these verses speak primarily to the relationships we share with one another is made very clear when verse three is read.

> He is like a tree planted firmly by streams of water, that yields its fruit in its season, and its leaf does not wither. In all that he does, he prospers (Ps 1:3).

There is much to learn from this single verse. First of all, a person does not become "firmly planted" through self-will and self-determination. The "planting" comes only after a commitment to avoid all dimensions of sinful activity (verse 1), and a commitment to become intimately involved in the divine will (verse 2), appropriating that will until it becomes second nature.

In the New Testament, we find that James also teaches the importance of following God's will rather than our own.

> Come now, you who say, "Today or tomorrow we will go into such and such a town and spend a year there and trade and get

gain"; whereas you do not know about tomorrow. What is your life? For you are a mist that appears for a little time and then vanishes. Instead you ought to say, "If the Lord wills, we shall live and we shall do this or that." As it is, you boast in your arrogance. All such boasting is evil (James 4:13-16).

A conscious decision must be made concerning the divine will, but apart from God Himself, no amount of conscious decision-making is going to make any difference. In other words, there is no becoming like a tree planted firmly by the water if there is no water by which to become planted.

Although Revelation 22 refers to a time when all things become new, the expressed truths are no less sound during these final days in which we are living, namely, that God is the source of all sustenance which is true and enduring.

Then he showed me the river of the water of life, bright as crystal, flowing from the throne of God and of the Lamb through the middle of the street of the city; also, on either side of the river, the tree of life with its twelve kinds of fruit, yielding its fruit each month; and the leaves of the tree were for the healing of the nations. There shall no more be anything accursed, but the throne of God and of the Lamb shall be in it, and his servant shall worship him; they shall see his face, and his name shall be on their foreheads. And night shall be no more; they need no light of lamp or sun, for the Lord God will be their light, and they shall reign for ever and ever (Rev 22:1-5).

These five verses clearly depict God as the Giver of Life, the One who will once again provide the Tree of Life to those willing to receive its sustenance. But as these verses are read alongside Psalm 1, some very interesting parallels result, parallels which have everything to do with our God-given responsibility to care for one another.

Since humanity was driven from the garden of Eden, the Tree of Life has been inaccessible (Gen 3:22-24). Revelation 22 testifies of its re-appearance, nourished by the water of life, "flowing from the throne of God and of the Lamb." But more important than the future re-appearance of the Tree are the words concerning the "Tree of Life" found in Psalm 1.

Here, the "Tree of Life" is spoken of in present-tense terms, existing in the form of people who have appropriated God's will to the point where God's nature is internalized. These people are likened to trees, being strong themselves, possessing leaves which do not wither. But these are also people who bear fruit that others might benefit from their strength. Only then do people fulfil the purpose for which they are created and which is willed for them by God.

Speaking in the context of false prophets, but demonstrating again that "good fruit" is produced by those whose relationship with God is as it should be, Jesus' recorded words in Matthew 7 say,

> You will know them by their fruits. Are grapes gathered from thorns, or figs from thistles? So, every sound tree bears good fruit, but the bad tree bears evil fruit. A sound tree cannot bear evil fruit, nor can a bad tree bear good fruit. Every tree that does not bear good fruit is cut down and thrown into the fire. Thus you will know them by their fruits (Matt 7:16-20).

Matthew 7 goes further than Psalm 1 by suggesting that fruit is always born, whether it be evil fruit or good fruit. But Matthew and the psalmist agree that those living their lives in accordance with God's purpose will provide benefit to those around them by the production of fruit.

God feeds those who have dedicated themselves to His will, that they might be strong enough to nourish others. As the Tree of Life in Revelation 22 provides "healing," so do the "blessed" of God in this world provide healing to those around them.

This perspective is peculiar to those who perceive God's activity primarily as that which is beneficial to them. These are people so self-centered, that they cannot fathom a "move of God" as being anything other than that which has value for them directly.

What a shame, because scripturally speaking, God often moves through one person that another person might benefit; God often interrupts the life of one person, moving directly upon him or her, that others might receive something God has to offer them.

Although there are many examples which could be offered, perhaps none speak more clearly to these truths than the person of Jeremiah. He was truly a man weak in himself, but strengthened by God that others might benefit from his call, a call of God that was anything but pleasurable.

Perseverance Is Required

If there is to be named one man besides Jesus most familiar with the difficulties associated with a relationship with God, it would be the prophet Jeremiah. But through all of the seemingly insurmountable trials Jeremiah faced, he remained keenly aware of the significance and the implications of that relationship. Many of Jeremiah's prophecies offer evidence bearing this out, but chapter 17, in a fashion reminiscent of Psalm 1, testifies, in a most lucid manner, the prophet's awareness.

> Thus says the LORD: Cursed is the man who trusts in man and makes flesh his arm, whose heart turns away from the LORD. He is like a shrub in the desert, and shall not see any good come. He shall dwell in the parched places of the wilderness, in an uninhabited salt land. Blessed is the man who trusts in the LORD, whose trust is the LORD. He is like a tree planted by water, that sends out its roots by the stream, and does not fear when heat comes, for its leaves remain green, and is not anxious in the year of drought, for it does not cease to bear fruit (Jer 17:5-8).

In the person of Jeremiah, there are many admirable traits. But what is perhaps most admirable, seen in chapter 17 and elsewhere, is Jeremiah's persistence concerning the bearing of fruit. In fact, a single verse that numbers among those verses most astounding in all the Bible is one spoken by the "weeping prophet" himself in chapter 25.

> For twenty-three years, from the thirteenth year of Josiah the son of Amon, king of Judah, to this day, the word of the LORD has come to me, and I have spoken persistently to you, but you have not listened (Jer 25:3).

On the surface, the message of this verse is directed at the stubborn refusal of the people of Judah to heed the word of the Lord. And whereas the people's stubbornness was in place for twenty-three years, what was also in place was the stubborn refusal of Jeremiah to give up on his calling. For all those years, the people of Judah closed their ears to Jeremiah's ministry, but Jeremiah continued to minister, doing his best to be fruitful.

Such staying power is rare, especially when we take into account the great amount of physical and emotional abuse Jeremiah suffered.

He was beaten, imprisoned, placed in the cistern, and shunned by his neighbors. His former friends even had a nickname for him, "Magor-missabib" (Jer 20:3), meaning, "Terror On Every Side." Apparently, Jeremiah had made a name for himself as one who brought nothing but bad news.

The physical and emotional difficulties did not leave Jeremiah unaffected. In chapter 15, a remorseful prophet utters the words,

> Woe is me, my mother, that you bore me, a man of strife and contention to the whole land! I have not lent, nor have I borrowed, yet all of them curse me (Jer 15:10).

We see the torment the prophet is feeling, but it is even more pronounced in chapter 20.

> Cursed be the day on which I was born! The day when my mother bore me, let it not be blessed! Cursed be the man who brought the news to my father, "A son is born to you," making him very glad. Let that man be like the cities which the LORD overthrew without pity; let him hear a cry in the morning and an alarm at noon, because he did not kill me in the womb; so my mother would have been my grave, and her womb for ever great. Why did I come forth from the womb to see toil and sorrow, and spend my days in shame? (Jer 20:14-18)

Given the fact that Jeremiah was as disturbed as he was about his calling and his life, it is truly remarkable that he was as persistent as he was in his willingness to answer the call God placed upon him. For years, Jeremiah offered guidance and hope, but no one listened. Jeremiah's ministry focused upon a people who looked with disdain upon him, his message and his God. Yet, the prophet persisted.

Obviously, he was not in the world to please himself, but to fulfill God's purpose. And that purpose had everything to do with an attempt to leave a mark on the lives of those around him.

Jeremiah's words in chapters 15 and 20 reveal a man whose experience with God, world and self was, at times, more than he could bear. But we should not for a moment interpret Jeremiah's depressed cries as those which betray weakness or apathy. On the contrary, the cries of Jeremiah speak of a man who cared too much, who felt life too deeply. They are cries which speak of a man whose perceptions concerning God's will and the world's tragic state were keen, but whose own sense of inadequacy regarding both, was even more penetrating.

People like Jeremiah, whose perceptions of God and world are unusually keen, are those who typically suffer more than others. Their sensitivity to God and to others exhibits a genuine concern regarding both. But, with this concern, there often times comes great internal distress. We see this in the prophet Jeremiah, and it is evident also in the prophet Elijah.

After Elijah challenged and defeated the 450 prophets of Baal in 1 Kings 18, he slew them at the brook Kishon, and outraced King Ahab to Jezreel. When in Jezreel, one of Jezebel's messengers approached Elijah with the promise that Elijah would die as did the 450.

When the prophet heard this, he ran to Beersheba, then traveled a day's journey into the wilderness, sat under a juniper tree and requested of God that his life come to an end. "It is enough; now, O LORD, take away my life; for I am no better than my fathers" (1 Kgs 19:4). Elijah's words reveal an inner turmoil, one undoubtedly delivered to him by his ministry-related activities.

Elijah's victory over the prophets of Baal was tremendous and clearly, the moment was extraordinary. But, at the same time, it forced

Elijah to confront the very things most disturbing to him, most notably the people's distance from God, their disloyalty, selfishness, and idolatry. Elijah's victory was great, but its scope served to measure the depths of the depravity by which the prophet was surrounded. This, in addition to Jezebel's threat, was more than the prophet could bear.

From an examination of Jeremiah and Elijah, we can conclude that depression is not always a sign of weakness. Feelings of despair, uncertainty and discouragement sometimes serve to measure the extent to which we care, the breadth of our concern, the range of our "God-like interests."

In a very real sense, if a person is sensitive, both to God's expectations and to His people's shortcomings concerning those expectations, it is then reasonable for that person to be concerned, to feel inadequate, to express despair. This is certainly true where Elijah and Jeremiah are concerned. Therefore, if we, at times, have feelings similar to these, we are in good company.

Jeremiah's Templegate Sermon

Jeremiah was acutely aware of God's expectations, and therefore, the need for spiritual reform. Perhaps chapter 7 makes this clearer than any other portion of Jeremiah. It is a powerful chapter that accomplishes much, but perhaps most importantly, it makes clear the need for relationships in this world to be more than cursory, more than obligatory.

In chapter 7, we find the prophet standing at the templegate, a place where worshippers pass, those who proclaim to be devoted followers of the Lord. It is at this place and to these people that Jeremiah says,

> Hear the word of the LORD, all you men of Judah who enter these gates to worship the LORD. Thus says the LORD of

> hosts, the God of Israel, Amend your ways and your doings, and I will let you dwell in this place. Do not trust in these deceptive words: This is the temple of the LORD, the temple of the LORD, the temple of the LORD (Jer 7:2-4).

The first thing that must be concluded about these worshippers is that they were displeasing to God. Clearly, entering the temple to worship was not, in and of itself, something that impressed God. Apparently, these people attended temple services because it was "expected" of them. Worship had become a convention, a form, something done to fulfill societal, and perhaps familial expectations. But there was more to be said by Jeremiah.

> Will you steal, murder, commit adultery, swear falsely, burn incense to Baal, and go after other gods that you have not known, and then come and stand before me in this house, which is called by my name, and say, "We are delivered!"--only to go on doing all these abominations? Has this house, which is called by my name, become a den of robbers in your eyes? (Jer 7:9-11)

We look at these words and see the same attitude prevailing among the people of Judah as that attitude among the people in Micah's prophesy. In fact, the words of Jeremiah reveal a people who do more than ignore the needs of their neighbors; they actually disregard their needs, acting as though they are non-existent.

There is thievery, bearing false witness, even adultery and murder. And Jeremiah cannot believe that God's laws are being broken in such a cavalier fashion. There is the gross mistreatment of people and shortly following, an unremorseful participation in worship services. Such behavior can emanate only from a spirit of excessive arrogance, and such haughtiness cannot be looked upon by God with any measure of tolerance.

At the templegate, Jeremiah, speaking as the very voice of God, addresses a major problem concerning the people, a problem that has everything to do with relationships. This problem exists among the people, and in a simultaneous fashion, extends into the people's relationship with God. In the same behavior, there is inhumanity and a cold indifference to God and His laws. But the attitude towards God extends beyond that of indifference.

From Jeremiah's own words, the people abuse, even kill one another, then "come and stand before [God] in [His] house, which is called by [His] name, and say, `We are delivered!'" (Jer 7:10) The people are doing three things: (1) they are mistreating one another in a most inhumane manner, (2) in the process, they are breaking God's commandments, and (3) as they break God's commandments, they show their disregard, even their contempt, for God and His laws.

What could be more offensive to God than these three things coupled with a belief that absolution is granted because of participation in temple services? What could be more insulting to God than when a person breaks His laws in a most heinous manner, then enters His house, arrogantly expecting to be absolved of all wrong-doing?

It is a disturbing scene at the templegate. But it should be even more disturbing when we realize that it is a reflection of contemporary society as well. All too often, church participation becomes a gesture, an activity that grants opportunity for posturing, which is the same as pretense. With all too much frequency, people go to church, stand in the "right place," say the "right words," and do the "right things." And after doing so, they exit the sanctuary with their souls crying the words, "We are delivered! We are absolved!" And all this because they entered the Lord's house on His day.

Contemporary society would do well to remember the warning of God given through His prophet Jeremiah:

> Has this house, which is called by my name, become a den of robbers in your eyes? Behold, I myself have seen it, says the LORD. Go now to my place that was in Shiloh, where I made my name dwell at first, and see what I did to it for the wickedness of my people Israel (Jer 7:11-12).

The presence of the temple was not going to save the people of Jerusalem any more than the presence of the tabernacle in Shiloh saved the people during the time of the judges. In other words, the temple and its accompanying rituals, by themselves, had absolutely nothing to do with redemption.

The same applies today, for it is not the church building, or the various displays associated with it that necessarily please God in any manner. Unlike people, God is not misled or deceived by "tactics" and "exhibitions." God looks upon the heart and judges the person according to what is seen there.

The church building is a gathering point. It is a place where like-minded people assemble with a sincere desire to praise and worship God, but also to provide and receive support and encouragement regarding efforts to serve God and advance in His grace. The worship services are not in place that people might impress or delude, but that there might be growth, growth in regard to God, and growth in regard to one another.

If church participation is not predicated upon these things, then God's desire is for participation to cease. This is basically the message found in Joshua 24. Joshua was speaking to the people of Israel, but his words are also a message for the people of God in all generations.

Now, therefore fear the LORD, and serve him in sincerity and in faithfulness; put away the gods which your fathers served beyond the River, and in Egypt, and serve the LORD. And if you be unwilling to serve the LORD, choose this day whom you will serve, whether the gods your fathers served in the region beyond the River, or the gods of the Amorites in whose land you dwell; but as for me and my house, we will serve the LORD (Josh 24:14-15).

The message is simple in that it calls for a decision. It is not unlike the words spoken by Elijah in 1 Kings 18 before he challenged the 450 prophets of Baal to a contest.

How long will you go limping with two different opinions? If the LORD is God, follow him; but if Baal, then follow him (1 Kgs 18:21).

Translated differently, "How long will you hesitate between two opinions?" Or, "How long will you jump between two forks?" Jeremiah knew it, as did Joshua and Elijah. And now, we must know it. No person can serve two gods without lying to one of them. Therefore, a decision must be made as to whom we will serve.

The time must come in our lives when we cease in our attempt to keep all options open. There comes a time when maturity demands that decisions be made, decisions concerning loyalty and values. And let us not think for a moment that anything less than our entire self will be accepted by God, for anything less is pretentious and therefore, completely unacceptable.

It may be helpful at this point, and somewhat comforting, to recognize that Jeremiah did not begin as a devoted man of God. And we need look no further than his initial response to God's calling to see this. Jeremiah heard the words,

> Before I formed you in the womb I knew you, and before you were born I consecrated you; I appointed you a prophet to the nations (Jer 1:5).

The clear call of God came to Jeremiah, but Jeremiah's immediate response was to reject it by offering excuses: "Ah, Lord God! Behold, I do not know how to speak, for I am only a youth" (Jer 1:6).

While it is true that anyone would have hesitated under similar conditions, the point is that Jeremiah became a mature man of God through a process. It did not happen overnight and it did not happen without trial and difficulty. But it did happen. And though there are many portions of Scripture that attest to this, perhaps the most poignant is in chapter 25, for only a mature man of God could have said,

> For twenty-three years, from the thirteenth year of Josiah the son of Amon, king of Judah, to this day, the word of the LORD has come to me, and I have spoken persistently to you, but you have not listened (Jer 25:3).

All Christians, at one time or another, feel inadequate concerning their relationship with God. One of the more discouraging conclusions to which any person can come is that they are failing God, or that they will never measure up.

One thing is certain. Every person is inadequate. But, fortunately, at least two more certainties remain: (1) God is accepting of us as we are, and (2) it is only through a process, that we learn to serve God and truly become someone more than we once were.

We must not forget the significance of the difficulties and the mistakes and the struggles. Apart from them, we cannot possibly learn and grow, becoming those people who are pleasing in the sight of God. Understanding and accepting the "process" is beyond important. It is that which shapes and defines us in accordance with God's will.

Jeremiah was called of God that he might minister to the people of this world. And this is exactly what he did. He influenced the lives of others as he followed his calling. Interestingly enough, from an earthly perspective, Jeremiah was unsuccessful, for no one listened, and no lives were changed. But from God's vantage point, Jeremiah was tremendously successful.

No one listened, but Jeremiah made the attempt. No one reaped benefit from what Jeremiah had to offer, but the fruit was made available. Jeremiah suffered greatly, and people shunned his very presence. But Jeremiah did as God expected him to do.

Jeremiah demonstrates a staying power that is rare. Every day presented the prophet with another reason to resign his commission, but he chose to see each new day as another opportunity to turn things around. No person needs search very far for a reason to quit. It is always much more difficult to find a reason to continue. But Jeremiah did exactly that, every day, for more than forty years.

In all that time, Jeremiah never accomplished what God would have him concerning the people of Judah. But he did manage to accomplish a great deal regarding his own relationship with God. He began his ministry opposed to God's expectations. And along the way, he still encountered personal battles with those expectations. But in the end, he was more "like God" than most of us will ever become.

This is evidenced by two things: (1) his unselfish concern for other people seen primarily in his willingness to suffer that they might benefit, and (2) his "God-like" qualities which developed, most notably his persistence. As Jeremiah's association with God continued, the transformation of the prophet progressed further and further.

There is nothing more important for Christians in our society to see than an association with God always brings transformation to the relationships we share with one another. Only the combination of these two give us our "God-like" character. As we look to the person of Moses, we will see further that an association with God always progresses in tandem with our earthly relationships. They simply cannot proceed in an independent fashion.

Anyone Can Change

Moses provides encouragement to most people in that his beginnings were something less than praiseworthy. Not only was he a murderer (Exod 2:12), but his initial response to God's calling was one of rejection. God speaks to him from the burning bush saying,

> I have seen the affliction of my people who are in Egypt, and have heard their cry because of their taskmasters; I know their sufferings, and I have come down to deliver them out of the hand of the Egyptians, and to bring them up out of that land to a good and broad land, a land flowing with milk and honey, to the place of the Canaanites, . . . Come, I will send you to Pharaoh that you may bring forth my people, the sons of Israel, out of Egypt (Exod 3:7-10).

From these words, there is no question that God descended to the earth that He and Moses might work to secure the release of the Israelites from the hands of Pharaoh. But, Moses was not interested. He responded, "Who am I that I should go to Pharaoh, and bring the sons of Israel out of Egypt?" (Exod 3:11)

At first, it may appear as though Moses truly felt unworthy to participate in such an undertaking. But, when Moses objects to his calling seven more times (Exod 3:13; 4:1, 10, 13; 5:22-23; 6:12, 30), it becomes clear that Moses was simply not interested. At this particular time in his life, he was not interested in pleasing God or serving humanity. His primary concern was for himself. But as the story progresses further, this changes dramatically.

While Moses is on Mount Sinai in chapter 32, God informs him that the people have constructed a golden calf.

> Go down; for your people, whom you brought up out of the land of Egypt, have corrupted themselves; they have turned aside quickly out of the way which I commanded them; they have made for themselves a molten calf, and have worshiped it and sacrificed to it, and said "These are your gods, O Israel, who brought you up out of the land of Egypt! . . I have seen this people, and behold, it is a stiff-necked people; now therefore let me alone, that my wrath may burn hot against them and I may consume them; but of you I will make a great nation (Exod 32:7-10).

God's anger produced an opportunity for Moses to be rid of the people of Israel. And Moses could be free with a clear conscience, for it would be God's doing, not his. But, a different Moses has emerged. He does not take advantage of the situation and "accept" God's words. Instead, Moses pleads with God on the people's behalf.

> O LORD, why does thy wrath burn hot against thy people, whom thou hast brought forth out of the land of Egypt with great power and with a mighty hand? Why should the Egyptians say, "With evil intent did he bring them forth, to slay

them in the mountains, and to consume them from the face of the earth"? Turn from thy fierce wrath, and repent of this evil against thy people" (Exod 32:11-12).

The Exodus material makes it clear that Moses prayed on behalf of the people of Israel, but only Deuteronomy informs us that Moses' intercession was for forty days and forty nights (Deut 9:25), revealing how difficult and sincere were the prayers of Moses. Indeed, Moses had changed.

Moses' allegiance to the people of Israel is even more evident when a subtlety is observed in the interchange between Moses and God. When God addresses Moses in Exodus 32:7, God refers to the people, not as "my" people, but as "thy" people. This is significant, because up until now, God was very possessive of the people, referring to them as His own. Seemingly, God has already separated Himself from them.

Moses notices the change in pronouns, and responds to God by reminding Him that the people still belong to Him. Speaking to God, it is now Moses' turn to refer to the people as "thy" people (Exod 32:11). It appears as though God and Moses are reminding one another of their mutual responsibilities while, at the same time, attempting to absolve themselves of the same.

Much could be said about this interchange between God and Moses, but what remains clear is that Moses was unwilling to leave God's presence until "the LORD repented of the evil which he thought to do to his people" (Exod 32:14). In other words, Moses' prayers were effective to the point where the mind of God was changed concerning the fate of an entire nation.

Whereas the text makes plain that Moses' prayers effected a major shift in God's plans, what is also true is that God "set Moses up" by announcing His plans. In a very real sense, God "delayed" the destruction of the people that Moses might be tested, that Moses' progress might be measured.

When speaking to Moses, God opened a door. "Now therefore let me alone, that my wrath may burn hot against them and I may consume them." And then to make it all even more tempting, "but of you I will make a great nation" (Exod 32:10). But, Moses remained, proving his loyalty to God and His calling, and at the same time, demonstrating a concern for those around him. Once again, we see that Moses' association with God developed concurrently with his association with God's people.

Moses had come a long way since his eight objections to God's calling. But as we chart Moses' life, we see that, like Jeremiah, maturity did not come easily for him. In fact, in both lives, we see that maturity came only as difficulties were overcome, as though they were a necessary part of the process.

For Moses, what was perhaps the greatest challenge was to transcend the results of his own sin at Kadesh. This was undoubtedly his mostly costly transgression in that it cost him entrance into the Land of Promise. Numbers 20 recounts the events leading up to and surrounding his sin.

After the people complain bitterly about the lack of food and water (Num 20:5), God speaks to Moses saying,

> Take the rod, and assemble the congregation, you and Aaron your brother, and tell the rock before their eyes to yield its water; so you shall bring water out of the rock for them; so you shall give drink to the congregation and their cattle (Num 20:8).

The instructions are simple enough. Moses is to (1) take the rod (which has now become a symbol for God), (2) assemble the people, and (3) speak to the rock. However, Moses follows his own agenda.

> And Moses and Aaron gathered the assembly together before the rock, and he said to them, "Hear now, you rebels; shall we bring forth water for you out of this rock?" And Moses lifted up his hand and struck the rock with his rod twice; and water came forth abundantly, and the congregation drank, and the cattle (Num 20:10-11).

Moses followed the first of God's instructions, but that was as far as he went. He assembled the congregation of Israel, but instead of speaking to the rock as God instructed, he spoke to the people, and then in anger, struck the rock.

The text gives every indication that God's intention was to quench the people's thirst, thereby restoring their faith in His ability to care for them. Therefore, Moses allowed his own anger and frustration to undermine, even sabotage what was meant to be a benevolent and life-giving act. Following his own base impulses, Moses turned the situation into an opportunity to berate and censure the people. Needless to say, God was not pleased. He spoke to Moses and said,

> Because you did not believe in me, to sanctify me in the eyes of the people of Israel, therefore you shall not bring this assembly into the land which I have given them (Num 20:12).

It is not unimportant that the first thing God told Moses to do was to "take the rod" (Num 20:8), for the rod had become a symbol of God himself. Therefore, God's desire was for the people to see that He was responsible for what was about to happen. But Moses' actions completely transformed God's intention.

In verse 11, Moses does not raise the rod but his hand, focusing attention upon himself rather than God. And in what can only be construed as an act of defiance, Moses, instead of speaking to the rock as God commanded, strikes the rock, and does so twice. By using the rod to strike the rock, Moses creates the impression that God is angry, and that water is provided only under protest.

Clearly, Moses took advantage of the situation to carry out his own agenda. And though it is not communicated in the text, it most certainly devastated Moses to be denied access into the Promised Land, especially since the punishment was deserved. But instead of quitting, Moses went forward, learning from his mistake rather than wallowing in the painful results. And, as demonstrated in Exodus 32, he eventually arrived at a place where his behavior before God and people testified of a character that had "God-like" proportions.

Moses speaks to those people who continue to re-live a past mistake. All too often, people do exactly this, dwelling on the things that should have been or could have been, allowing the things that are "not" to inhibit and obstruct, rather than working to deepen and enhance the things that "are."

Like Moses, we need to take even our most distressful experiences and use them in a way that is beneficial rather than detrimental. We need to remember that there is no experience God would not have us move beyond. And there is no sin that God would have inhibit or restrict us, for God's desire is for His people to always move forward. The consequences of sin may not always be alleviated, as in Moses' case, but God's desires for His people remain the same. And as are the desires of God, so must ours be concerning ourselves and others.

It has already been said that the rod of Moses is symbolic of divine power, even God himself. But interestingly enough, the "rod" or "staff" of Moses is also used, in an underlying fashion, to direct the reader's attention to the transformation of Moses' character that is taking place.

Moses obviously retains his humanity throughout the story, but at the same time, as Moses remains in contact with God, associating himself with God's will and expectations, the prophet becomes more than he once was. From God's own mouth, Moses' character transcends that which is solely of this earth.

> On the day when the LORD spoke to Moses in the land of Egypt, the LORD said to Moses, "I am the LORD; tell Pharaoh king of Egypt all that I say to you." But Moses said to the LORD, "Behold, I am of uncircumcised lips; how then shall Pharaoh listen to me?" And the LORD said to Moses, "*See, I make you as God to Pharaoh; and Aaron your brother shall be your prophet*" (Exod 6:28-7:1).

Granted, God is responsible for giving Moses the authority that is his, but it remains an authority that rivals that of Pharaoh himself. And Pharaoh is more than king; he is the very personification of evil.

At the initial confrontation between Moses and Pharaoh, the rod of Moses is used to defeat the magic of Pharaoh's sorcerers. As the story progresses beyond this introductory conflict, the rod, a symbol of God's power, becomes "confused" with Moses' hand, an ambiguity that bears witness to the development of Moses' stature.

This "deliberate ambiguity" is seen most plainly in chapter 14 at the Red Sea where Moses' conflict with Pharaoh is at a climax.

The LORD said to Moses, "Why do you cry to me? Tell the people of Israel to go forward. Lift up *your rod*, and stretch out *your hand* over the sea and divide it, that the people of Israel may go on dry ground through the sea" (Exod 14:15-16).

It is clear that the rod of God and the hand of Moses play an equally important, seemingly interchangeable role at this point, thus demonstrating Moses' transformation. But even more telling is Exodus 14:31 where God and Moses are paralleled as the single object of Israel's belief.

In this verse, the people of Israel saw the great work of the Lord regarding the Egyptians and "they believed in the LORD and in his servant Moses." Now, there is more than a parallel between Moses' hand and that which is a symbol of God; clearly, the person of Moses is identified with God Himself.

As mentioned at the beginning of this section, Moses provides us with much encouragement. He is as human as they come, subject to frailty and hesitancy and fear. Indeed, he is a sinful man, in need of much refinement, yet the call of God is given.

And what is even more encouraging is that Moses' imperfections continue to be exhibited even after an acceptance of his calling. From this we learn that spiritual development does not need a sinless vacuum in order to exist. In fact, it could be said that human failing is the breeding ground for spiritual maturation. In a very real sense, for the latter to exist, there must first be the former. And that is indeed good news for every person.

Traveling Beyond Grace

Any person having even minimal familiarity with scriptural content is aware of the many riches contained therein. Unfortunately, these same people, all too often, allow the limits of their own minds to mark the extent to which Scriptures can take them.

When this occurs, the Bible is less able to shape and inform the reader. Instead, Scriptures function to substantiate a belief structure that has already been formed. If terrestrial limitations determine the boundaries of truth and meaning, then transcendent reality lies just beyond our grasp. And the portion of the Bible's message having its origin in the mind of God is hopelessly elusive.

It is not uncommon for a reader's world to be so compelling, that scriptural statements are routinely "disallowed" when they disagree with those things previously embraced. An example arises from the Sermon on the Mount.

> You have heard that it was said to the men of old, "You shall not kill; and whoever kills shall be liable to judgment." But I say to you that every one who is angry with his brother shall be liable to the council, and whoever says, "You fool!" shall be liable to the hell of fire (Matt 5:21-22).

Creative interpretations often abound when these verses are encountered because of two common convictions: (1) it is not possible for a person to be as respectful of others as these verses indicate, and/or (2) such a punishment cannot result from such a "minor" infraction of God's expectations. In one way or another, it is concluded that Jesus' words are "consciously exaggerated" for the purpose of making a point.

It is not uncommon for readers to disrupt the integrity of God's Word on a subconscious level. Because "truth" is processed from within a particular reality, some "corruption" is inevitable. But while a measure of forgiveness must be offered, what must remain is the unacceptability of disregarding, overlooking, and being otherwise inattentive to words which are meant to re-shape, and re-define our thinking and our value-structure, therefore, our very existence.

At times, readers "overlook" certain scriptural portions in an effort to protect their "worlds." At other times, scriptural truths remain undiscovered simply because readers are unable to reconcile these truths with their pre-existing belief structure. There is a difference in that the former occurs on a more conscious level than the latter. But in both cases, there is difficulty accepting that which is "unfamiliar."

One example arises from a portion of 2 Peter.

> His divine power has granted to us all things that pertain to life and godliness, through the knowledge of him who called us to his own glory and excellence, by which he has granted to us his precious and very great promises, that through these you may escape from the corruption that is in the world because of passion, and become *partakers of the divine nature* (2 Pet 1:3-4).

People commonly do one of two things with the phrase, "partakers of the divine nature." They either (1) apply the words to the future, when all things will become new, or (2) they understate the significance and therefore, the extent to which participation in the divine nature is presently possible.

As demonstrated in the person of Moses, a transformation of the human nature takes place as an association with God persists and as human effort is exerted. Furthermore, this transformation occurs in concert with a progression of one's ability to relate to other people in a "God-like" fashion. Concerning Moses, there was, at first, an indifference to the needs of others. But eventually, Moses' character became so transformed that he was willing to forfeit his own life that the lives of others might continue.

That "participation in the divine nature" has much to do with the way we relate to one another is affirmed by the message which follows Peter's declaration concerning that participation. After this declaration, Peter says,

> For this very reason make every effort to supplement your faith with virtue, and virtue with knowledge, and knowledge with self-control, and self-control with steadfastness, and steadfastness with godliness, and godliness with brotherly affection, and brotherly affection with love (2 Pet 1:5-7).

Clearly, there exists an undeniable nexus between the assimilation of the divine nature and the possession of certain qualities. And somewhat remarkably, the majority of the qualities mentioned pertain to the relationships shared with one another rather than the relationship shared with God. This reminds us, once again, that no clear point of demarcation exists between a person's relationship with God and the relationships shared with those in this world. Beyond question, they run a similar, if not identical course.

2 Peter indicates the need for human effort concerning these virtues. We, as the people of God, are called upon to "make every effort to add to our faith virtue, knowledge, self-control, etc. While God is willing to provide assistance to any person desirous of such noble virtues, He does not simply provide them upon request.

God has exerted effort through His Son Jesus Christ and unquestionably, there is no opportunity to become partakers of the divine nature apart from the divine effort. But, at the same time, human effort is also required. Jesus Christ makes possible the salvation, but the Christian must work out that salvation with "fear and trembling" (Phil 2:12). And according to Peter, part of that process involves the incorporation of several virtues into our lives. These qualities deserve a brief examination.

The first quality Peter mentions after "faith" is "virtue," which is a classic term from greek ethics. It is easily translated, "excellence," and probably refers to excellence regarding practical goodness. In other words, Christians are called upon to daily fulfill that which is the most excellent part of humanity. Business transactions, encounters with strangers, dealings with family and everything else that comprises a person's day, must reflect an expenditure of energy which testifies of an association with God that is not only genuine, but life-changing.

After "virtue," Peter mentions the need for "knowledge." Clearly, this places a constraint upon Christians to attend to the intellectual portion of themselves. But Peter does not have in mind the kind of knowledge that is content-oriented. On the contrary, Christians are expected to strive for knowledge that grants them insight concerning very practical matters. In other words, God's people must work at becoming knowledgeable in the Lord in order that they might know the difference between what is right and what is wrong.

This sounds very elementary, but the fact of the matter is that many people, including those who are Christians, spend far too much time extricating themselves from circumstances in which they should never have found themselves in the first place. There are always explanations ranging from an unawareness of hidden snares to being just plain ignorant. But regardless of the explanations offered, what cannot be denied is that these situations would have been avoided if there was "knowledge" and an accompanying desire to allow that knowledge to guide behavior.

By associating with God and His Word, Christians become "knowledgeable" to the point where they are able to rationalize that which is proper and that which is improper. The possession of "knowledge" allows a person to weigh alternatives, and formulate conclusions. The Bible does not always address a particular issue with the kind of specificity we are comfortable with. But when Christians associate themselves with God and with God's Word, "knowledge" springs forth, and with it, an ability to distinguish between that which is right and that which is wrong.

As we move through Peter's list, we come next to the call for "self-control." Self-control makes reference to many things. Without question, Peter has in mind the various human appetites, but perhaps more than anything else, Peter is speaking to human passion and lust.

Now, at this point, it is important to stop and realize that Peter is calling for *Christians* to control their lusts and their passions. Strangely enough, there are some who say that lusts and passions become an "unnatural" part of a person's life once Christ enters in. But Peter gives no indication of this. There is no question that Peter calls for Christians to control this portion of their humanity. But at the same time, it is important to note that there is not even a hint at the need for its obliteration. Peter speaks only to the importance of *controlling* the human appetites.

No rational Christian person would dispute the importance of "self-control," for herein lies an essential element for standing firmly when confronted by temptation. Just as there are endless possibilities for the daily display of Christian virtues, so is there boundless potential for sin. And with "self-control," a person may master the sin that lies crouching at every door.

The next quality in Peter's list is that of "steadfastness," which can also be translated as "endurance" or "patience." "Steadfastness" is the temper of the mind which is unmoved by difficulty. Having already examined this quality in the person of Jeremiah, we have been exposed to a practical view of its quality.

We must understand that "steadfastness" is not some stoic acceptance of pain and trial. On the contrary, "steadfastness" is that which springs from faith. It is found in the person who has fixed his mind, not on the inconsistencies of life, but on the steady, unfailing consistencies of God. This quality is found, not in the person who relies upon miraculous displays or emotions, but in the person who places his confidence upon God's work, God's majesty, and God's love, for these always have been, and forever will remain.

The next virtue in Peter's list is that of "godliness," sometimes translated, "reverence." The word is rarely found in the Bible, but relates to a person who fulfills his obligations to God. It speaks of a person who is careful and correct in performing spiritual duties, regardless of the results or the rewards. Again, Jeremiah provided us with ample illustration of a person possessing "godliness."

Certainly, every person is unique in the sense that there are different duties to perform and distinct obligations to fulfill. But, as has been maintained from the beginning of this chapter, there is one general responsibility to God we all share and that is the one related directly to the responsibility we have to one another. Treating one another in a "God-like" manner portrays the very essence of being reverent to God. It is the sum and substance of "godliness" and is indisputably required of every Christian person.

If the virtues in 2 Peter 1 necessarily build upon one another, the latter two qualities then become, not only the most difficult to attain, but the most significant in terms of Christian achievement. From the material presented thus far, it should not be surprising to discover that the last two virtues speak most pointedly to the relationships we share with one another in this world. These final qualities are "brotherly affection" and "love." They are so similar, they will be spoken of as though they are one.

The next chapter carries a more detailed discussion of "love" but let it be said for now that "love" is the distinguishing mark of true discipleship. It means that we, like Moses, have a concern for one another that exceeds the concern we have for ourselves. It means we guard Spirit-given unity by refusing to slander and belittle one another. And it means we carry that love for other people even if we receive none in return.

A "God-like" love is that which exists all by itself. That is to say, it is a love that requires no response, for no return is either needed or expected. Possessing God's kind of love means, among other things, that no object is necessary. Very simply, it is a love that "is" and remains no matter what.

Unfortunately, the possession of such love is much more the exception than it is the norm. All too often, people immediately think of themselves, habitually processing information that potential benefit to self might be calculated. For the majority of people, the world flows but in a single direction, this being to themselves.

After Peter lists these virtues, he offers words which bring tremendous significance to the effort required to possess and sustain these qualities.

> For if these things are yours and abound, they keep you from being ineffective or unfruitful in the knowledge of our Lord Jesus Christ. For whoever lacks these things is blind and shortsighted and has forgotten that he was cleansed from his old sins. Therefore, brethren, be the more zealous to confirm your call and election, for if you do this you will never fall; *so there will be richly provided for you an entrance into the eternal kingdom of our Lord and Savior Jesus Christ* (2 Pet 1:8-11).

According to Peter, being in possession of the qualities mentioned keeps a person (1) from being ineffective and unfruitful, (2) from being blind and shortsighted, and most importantly, (3) from being denied entrance into God's kingdom. From Peter's words, there is plainly more required of Christians than faith in the Lord Jesus Christ. Peter's list of qualities BEGINS with faith, but clearly does not end there. It is an irrefutable fact that faith is an absolutely necessary component for Christianity, but what is also undeniable is that Christians are productive and something other than myopic in their "Christian" vision only when other qualities are added to that faith.

If we are to occupy this world in the manner God would have us, then we must be productive and effective, which means we must have something to offer those around us. If we "cocoon" ourselves, we do that which is decidedly NON-Christian, for God expects us to position ourselves in such a way that others see from our "God-like" character and behavior that we have something to offer. As we have already seen, our lives must bear fruit or they are not meeting the expectations of God.

Can it be true that our entrance into the eternal kingdom of God is predicated upon our Christian development beyond the point of conversion? Is it so difficult to understand that human effort is required in addition to the divine effort exerted by God through His Son Jesus Christ?

What has been presented thus far indicates an absolute need for people to develop beyond the point of initial belief. What God has made possible for His people, must, in a very real sense, be realized only through their efforts. Faith must be put into practice, or it is empty, beyond nothingness.

What does it profit, my brethren, if a man says he has faith but has not works? Can his faith save him? If a brother or sister is ill-clad and in lack of daily food, and one of you says to them, "Go in peace, be warmed and filled," without giving them the things needed for the body, what does it profit? So faith by itself, if it has no works, is dead (James 2:14-17).

As we shall see in even more detail in the chapters ahead, what is practiced and developed beyond the point of initial salvation has much to do with the relationships we share with one another. A proper relationship with God inescapably involves relationships with one another that are also proper and appropriate. This is what being "God-like" is all about.

It is only by relating to one another in a "God-like" manner that we become participants in the divine nature and have provided for us "an entrance into the eternal kingdom of our Lord and Savior Jesus Christ."

Pursue the endless story
Thread your way through the deceit
Then touch the walls of silence
Have no choice but to retreat

Many songs are sung beneath us
Heard through fissures formed by tears
The seams betray the struggle
Of the righteous through the years

Angels cast aside their virtues
Their crowns still mixed with gold
Confusion meets refreshment
And the warmth confronts the cold

Reaching through the darkened shadows
Forlorn spirits stay their hand
The messengers bring solace
Fading souls find room to stand
                    P.L. Engstrom

CHAPTER TWO
The Inner Transformation

The previous chapter presented scriptural evidence which makes it necessary for Christians to do more than express faith in Jesus Christ as the Savior of the world. Without question, this expression remains absolutely foundational for Christianity, but what also remains is the mandate concerning the incorporation of certain characteristics into the lives of those who profess such faith. Simply said, the relationships shared with one another must reflect, not only the relationship shared with God, but God Himself.

Some might question the coherence of such conclusions, maintaining that they are either unreasonable or the projection of utopian idealism. But, what cannot be denied is the clarity with which God's Word presents the conclusion offered. Consequently, those who question, either disbelieve clear scriptural teaching, or are so far removed from the transformation necessary to comprehend it, that they are simply incapable of doing so. As paradoxical as it might sound, it is likely that the limits of one's own world often serves as the greatest obstacle to that world in which God would have us live.

Individual worlds are uncontrollably varied as the diversity of experience shapes the contour of human development. But one thing people have in common is the need to escape whatever world is theirs and pierce through to the world that is God's. The possibility of such a move exists as the result of divine effort, but human effort is also necessary. Unfortunately, effort is something many people are unwilling to put forth. Instead, they wait expectantly, with their hands wide open.

Sloth Brings Defeat

There is a familiar story in John's gospel that portrays, among other truths, the tendency that lies within human nature to expect something for nothing, to expect reward for immobility.

Now there is in Jerusalem by the Sheep Gate a pool, in Hebrew called Bethzatha, which has five porticoes. In these lay a multitude of invalids, blind, lame, paralyzed. One man was there, who had been ill for thirty-eight years. When Jesus saw him and knew that he had been lying there a long time, he said to him, "Do you want to be healed?" The sick man answered him, "Sir, I have no man to put me into the pool when the water is troubled, and while I am going another steps down before me." Jesus said to him, "Rise, take up your pallet, and walk." And at once the man was healed, and he took up his pallet and walked (John 5:2-9).

The scene at the pool of Bethesda is, on the one hand, a picture of beneficence, compassion and power. But, on the other hand, the scene is a disturbing one. At this pool, we find thousands upon thousands of people gathered for a single purpose: to watch for the water's slightest movement.

Day after day, and we can only assume, night after night, these people fixed their gaze upon the pool, hoping to detect the slightest stirring, that they might leap into the pool ahead of thousands of others. Certainly, these people spent entire days poised selfishly over the pool on the brink of imbalance, that they might be the one to receive healing.

The imagery associated with the multitudes at the pool is reflective of people in every generation. It is not unusual for people to spend their lives so certain they have been slighted, so convinced they have been dealt some injustice, that, as they search for something more or something better, they lose sight of the present. These people are in danger of becoming so oblivious to the moment at hand, that their lives lose any significance that is already in their grasp. And when this occurs, God's intention for life--for it to be meaningful all by itself--is lost. And that loss has repercussions into eternity.

Endeavoring to attain something more is not necessarily destructive, but when present efforts are stalled as a result, there is incalculable, sometimes irretrievable loss. Inactivity has always been, and will forever remain the key ingredient necessary for life to be unfruitful and unproductive. And this is just as true, if not more so, where Christian development is concerned.

If Christians do nothing beyond the point of salvation, they have succeeded only in accepting the most significant, potentially life-changing gift this world has ever been offered. There is nothing praiseworthy here. In fact, such a lack of response is supremely insulting to God.

Unquestionably, salvation is a gift, but not one that is to be selfishly embraced. It is a gift meant to have repercussions through the entire world, and these repercussions only exist as believers carry the message beyond themselves, through words and behavior and lifestyles. In fact, it may be very accurate to say that salvation is eventually lost when those receiving the gift attempt to envelop it, shielding it from the view of others.

The Truth Is Identified

As Peter and James remind their readers that human effort is required beyond the point of salvation, so does Jesus offer the same instruction.

> Seeing the crowds, he went up on the mountain, and when he sat down his disciples came to him. And he opened his mouth and taught them, saying: Blessed are the poor in spirit, for theirs is the kingdom of heaven. Blessed are those who mourn, for they shall be comforted. Blessed are the meek, for they shall inherit the earth. Blessed are those who hunger and thirst for righteousness, for they shall be satisfied. Blessed are the merciful, for they shall obtain mercy. Blessed are the pure in heart, for they shall see God. Blessed are the peacemakers, for they shall be called sons of God. Blessed are those who are persecuted for righteousness' sake, for theirs is the kingdom of heaven. Blessed are you when men revile you and persecute you and utter all kinds of evil against you falsely on my

account. Rejoice and be glad, for your reward is great in heaven, for so men persecuted the prophets who were before you (Matt 5:1-11).

Matthew makes it clear in the first verse that Jesus spoke these words, not to the multitudes, but to His disciples. In other words, Jesus was not speaking to those who needed to be convinced about the reality of the kingdom of God, but to those who had already found it. And just as these words were spoken to those who had already "arrived," in Jesus' day, so do they speak to the people who have "arrived" in our day.

It is important to understand that these eight beatitudes do not make reference to eight different individuals, each one possessing a certain trait. On the contrary, they define the essential character of every person who follows Christ. Jesus defined what are to be the inherent qualities of every person professing Him as Savior.

As we look briefly at these beatitudes, we must remember that, as they speak to a Christian's responsibility to God, they also speak to the responsibility we have to one another. And perhaps what is more important is the recognition that these traits do not become ours by divine grace; they require effort, and admittedly, effort that is, at times, quite elusive.

"Blessed are the poor in spirit"

The first beatitude refers to being keenly aware of a need for God. As this type of humility is necessary at the point of salvation, so it remains an essential element in the post-salvation relationship.

When a person enters into a relationship with God, it is not uncommon for the scenario to be as follows: (1) some kind of "need" prompts a spiritual search, (2) this search results in a certain "awareness" of God, and (3) the new-found awareness leads to a conversion experience.

No immediate difficulty exists with people coming into salvation as the result of some crisis experience. But there is a potential complication in that when the crisis is past, there exists the possibility of spiritual reversal.

There are those who experience salvation only at some point to become self-sufficient again, needing, in their minds, no person and no thing. They refuse to turn to others for help, perceiving it as some kind of weakness. And in their refusal to turn to others, there exists a stubbornness that inevitably affects their relationship with God.

This mentality is the direct antithesis to being "poor in spirit," and is therefore incompatible with the kingdom of God. Only those who remain dependent on God's many graces remain heirs of His kingdom.

"Blessed are those who mourn"

The mourning to which Jesus refers has nothing to do with the grieving process one goes through when a loved one passes away. It has everything to do with the mourning and the lamenting that issues forth when there is an acute appreciation of one's own sin and failings.

What comes naturally for people is to discern the sins and the failings of others. The slightest error made by any other person is immediately recognized and then, to make matters worse, communicated to someone else. Perhaps this is a defense mechanism which allows people to remain less sensitive to their own inadequacies. But, whatever the reason, Christians must work to turn this tendency around, for it is anything but Christ-like.

Christian people must not become de-sensitized to their imperfections, for when this occurs, standards become more conformed to those set by the world than by God. God does not expect imperfect righteousness to stifle and inhibit His people. But at the same time, there must be an unwillingness to accept it. In other words, the people of God must put forth effort if they are to remain both "familiar" and "unfamiliar" with sin in their lives and, for that matter, with the evil that is so prevalent in the world. And being always mindful of its presence but removed from its effects, is a difficult tension to maintain.

"Blessed are the meek"

Meekness refers, not only to the humility to be practiced in our relationship with God, but to the humility that must govern the relationships we have with one another.

Basically, a person is meek before God as that person maintains an attitude of dependence upon Him. And humility before one another is accomplished as Christians practice the kind of love of which Paul speaks in 1 Corinthians 13. Much more will be said concerning this kind of love later, but let it be said for now that it is a love that MUST be practiced if it is to become a real part of a person's life.

Practicing the kind of love of which Paul speaks is one of the more difficult transformations Christians are expected to bring about in their lives. But without question, those who profess Christ as Savior are expected to practice such meekness before every other person. And herein lies much of the difficulty, because Christians are to be meek before those who, in their minds, "deserve" such treatment, but also before those whom they have determined do not.

Christians must work to "de-categorize" people, striving to see the soul instead of the differences and the errors. Making determinations and drawing conclusions is much more likely to cause factions than solidarity. And when this occurs, that for which Christians are expected to strive is lost.

Much more will be said about meekness and love later, but let the present summary statement be this: the person who is the greatest in the kingdom of God is the person who has humbled himself first before God, but then, before the thousands, even the millions.

"Blessed are those who hunger and thirst for righteousness"

Reading this beatitude in conjunction with the second reveals a very important truth concerning the Christian experience beyond salvation: we must work in two different directions to accomplish one thing.

The second beatitude reminds us of the importance of being aware of sin and evil, not that we might feel burdened and inhibited, but that we might work to overcome its effects. And while this is certainly sound instruction, what the fourth beatitude reminds us is that there must also be striving for the righteousness of God. This occurs through diligent prayer and Bible study, but also by striving to be people who daily do what is right and proper and appropriate in the sight of God. And as already discussed, this striving can only manifest itself in everyday relationships.

Hungering and thirsting after righteousness always involves effort concerning both sin and righteousness. But the efforts are different in the sense that we work to repel sin while we strive to embrace righteousness. Said another way, the effort to discard the old nature is coupled with the struggle to be clothed with the new.

"Blessed are the merciful"

In this beatitude, the mandatory nature of being merciful is expressed. Jesus teaches that in order to receive mercy, the same must be extended to others.

The mercy of God is continually offered, but only to those who incorporate an attitude of mercy themselves. And such a quality is immediately discernible in people. In their everyday behavior, they are accepting of those who do things differently, tolerant of those who require instruction, and forgiving of those who make mistakes.

In one sense, this beatitude is a reminder that people give to others what they themselves receive. And said another way, people treat others with the same measures of respect, compassion and charity which they themselves receive. What should be obvious but is often forgotten is that people receive exactly what they give.

Taking this further, it can be said that to receive insight concerning our treatment of others, we need only examine the way we are treated by others. Are people respectful and courteous and giving? Or are they inconsiderate, abusive and unforgiving?

There are always exceptions, but what is most often true is that our perceptions regarding the behavior of others are really observations concerning our own attitudes and behaviors, for people mirror back what they receive. And, interestingly enough, these observations carry an element of objectivity concerning ourselves that is normally quite elusive, because, as already discussed, the reality of our worlds are so compelling, that anything else is difficult to observe, let alone accept.

God takes all of this down a slightly different path in that He gives to His people exactly what they give to others. This beatitude speaks to a single area of a truth, but one that has more far-reaching effects. If God's people are merciful and forgiving and tolerant to others, then the same is extended to them by God.

> Judge not, that you be not judged. For with the judgment you pronounce you will be judged, and the measure you give will be the measure you get (Matt 7:1-2).

"Blessed are the pure in heart"

This beatitude is something, once again, for which the people of God must strive. And here, Jesus is not talking about righteousness, but the single-mindedness that springs from a heart determined to serve God with an allegiance that is undistracted and a devotion that is unwavering.

This is a difficult, if not varied task for the people of God. Even those who have accepted the salvation offered through Jesus Christ often have too many goals, too many desires, and too many masters. They allow their own agendas to pull them in directions which separate them from the path God has planned for their lives.

There is great difficulty when it comes to developing a devotion to God that is of a singular quality. And for every follower of Christ, there is a different route that must be taken, for there are always a different set of circumstances to overcome. There are obstacles from within and complications from without, but in whatever way necessary, they must be surmounted. Only then, does a person become what God expects. And only then is a person blessed.

"Blessed are the peacemakers"

In this beatitude, we find solid evidence concerning the need for Christians to develop their relationships with one another. The advancement of such a quality would certainly reflect the divine presence in this world, for Jesus Christ is nothing if not a reconciler.

Non-christians and Christians alike have difficulty when it comes to effectively reconciling those who are at odds with one another. It is sad commentary, but people are more capable of fanning a flame than they are extinguishing a fire.

One reason is that people are only capable of giving that which lies within them. Therefore, what a person can produce is only that which already exists. Although there are many able to bring harmony to a disorderly situation, there are many more who are only capable of fueling an already volatile situation. Often, this is due to an unresolved turmoil that lies within.

> Why do you see the speck that is in your brother's eye, but do not notice the log that is in your own eye? Or how can you say to your brother, "Let me take the speck out of your eye," when there is the log in your own eye? You hypocrite, first take the log out of your own eye, and then you will see clearly to take the speck out of your brother's eye (Matt 7:3-5).

These verses are relevant for the present discussion in that they indicate a person's inability to be "helpful" if his own life is in need of adjustment. How can there be sound counsel if it originates within a person who is himself unsound? Jesus teaches, "first take the log out of your own eye." When a person's own life is in order, great benefit can be brought to the life of another. Then, a person can become an effective peacemaker.

Additionally, these verses in Matthew 7 remind us of the tendency within people to do two things simultaneously: (1) judge their own behavior to be completely justifiable, and (2) find fault and deficiency as they observe the lives of others. It is not that people think themselves above reproach. The problem is that they justify their own behavior on whatever grounds without extending the same courtesy to others. Where the failings of others are concerned, it is concluded to be a simple matter of deficiency. And if this is not enough, the supposed shortcomings are then lifted up for many more to see. This puts into practice that which is directly opposed to the primary message of Christ, for this is when faults are discussed, weaknesses are uncovered, and failings are exposed.

According to this beatitude, a person who is a peacemaker will be called a "son of God." And if we understand this term to be equivalent to "member" of God, we are then brought back to the discussion concerning a Christian's "participation in the divine nature."

As God's followers work to reconcile the people of this world to God and to one another, there emerges a correspondence with the divine that is unmatched. Many names can be given Christ, but one that works well is "reconciler." And as we have seen, His people have been given the same responsibility, that Christ's work might continue.

> Therefore, if any one is in Christ, he is a new creation; the old has passed away, behold, the new has come. All this is from God, who through Christ reconciled us to himself and gave us the ministry of reconciliation; that is, God was in Christ reconciling the world to himself, not counting their trespasses against them, and entrusting to us the message of reconciliation. So *we are ambassadors for Christ, God making his appeal through us.* We beseech you on behalf of Christ, be reconciled to God. For our sake he made him to be sin who knew no sin, so that in him we might become the righteousness of God (2 Cor 5:17-21).

"Blessed are those who are persecuted for righteousness' sake"

This final beatitude follows up on the previous one in that it speaks about the inevitable persecution that comes to those who minister reconciliation. It is never easy to bring peace between God and others because, inevitably, much hurt surfaces. The same is true when there are attempts to resolve conflicts among people. Being "in the middle" is always a position of vulnerability.

This beatitude also speaks more generally in that it makes reference to people who are willing to uphold God's standards of truth, justice and purity. This world offers, on a routine basis, opposition to those who refuse to compromise their beliefs and their values. And if none is encountered, there is a good chance that re-evaluation is in order, for, generally speaking, persecution, in one form or another, will come to those who strive to participate in the divine nature.

These eight beatitudes indicate a sampling of traits to be incorporated into the lives of Christians. Clearly, human effort is necessary if believers are to fulfill the expectations of God. As we have seen repeatedly, an acceptance of Christ as Savior is only the beginning.

The difficulty and the effort associated with these beatitudes are both plainly visible, but the rewards associated with them must also be kept in view. If we are poor in spirit, the kingdom of heaven is ours. If we mourn the evil in the world and the sin in our own lives, we shall be comforted. If we are meek, seeking to maintain a humble spirit before God and humankind, we shall inherit the earth. If there is hungering and thirsting after righteousness, it will be found. If we are merciful and forgiving to those with whom we come in contact, the same will be given to us by God. If we establish a devotion to God that is single-minded, unswayed by the various distractions of life, we shall see God. If we are peacemakers, being those who bring reconciliation rather than division, there is real participation in divine effort. And even though criticism and condemnation are inevitable as the result of our efforts in this world, we are blessed, because the kingdom of heaven is in our grasp.

Salt and Light

As mentioned repeatedly, the eight beatitudes speak of the way in which we must relate to God. But they speak also of the way we are to relate to one another. This is clarified in the beatitudes themselves, but also in the words following them. Here, Jesus reminds His disciples what is to be their identity and position in the world.

> You are the salt of the earth; but if salt has lost its taste, how shall its saltness be restored? It is no longer good for anything except to be thrown out and trodden under foot by men. You are the light of the world. A city set on a hill cannot be hid. Nor do men light a lamp and put it under a bushel, but on a stand, and it gives light to all in the house. Let your light so shine before men, that they may see your good works and give glory to your Father who is in heaven (Matt 5:13-16).

Christians are salt in the sense that they are essentially different from the substance into which they are placed. In other words, followers of Christ are to act as moral disinfectants, arresting decay and preserving God-like principles. They are to transform the lives of those around them, not allow the lives of others to transform them.

Christians are light in that they reveal to the world that which must be known concerning God. By their words, attitudes, actions and deeds, followers of Christ allow what they have received to penetrate the darkness in such a way that "glory" is given to the "Father who is in heaven."

We must work to incorporate certain qualities into our lives that the person of God might be reflected in all that we say and do. As these traits become our own, lives are affected as we relate to people in a God-like manner. And earthly relationships must reflect our relationship with God. If they do not, then our relationship with God must be re-examined, for our associations with one another ALWAYS speak volumes regarding our association with God.

Some Things Must Die

Most people would agree that transformation is a natural accompaniment to the salvation experience. But the transformation that many have in mind is that which occurs on a spiritual level through Jesus Christ. And while there is no question that immaterial changes transpire through the grace of God, what must also be recognized is that the transformation is not complete at this point.

As already discussed, salvation is made possible through divine effort. But this is only the beginning. If it were both the beginning and the end of the process of salvation, the Bible would need not be so lengthy. As it turns out, much human effort is necessary as well. We have examined the beatitudes to receive some insight concerning this. But more insight is gained as we examine the third chapter of Paul's letter to the Colossians. Again, it will become clear that those who have accepted Christ have much more to accomplish.

Paul's opening words in Colossians 3 leave no doubt as to who his audience is. Clearly, he is speaking to those who know Jesus Christ as their personal savior, those who have already experienced the spiritual transformation that comes as the result of divine effort. What is also expressed is Paul's conviction, that in addition to human acceptance, there must be human effort.

> If then you have been raised with Christ, seek the things that are above, where Christ is, seated at the right hand of God. Set your minds on things that are above, not on things that are on earth. For you have died, and your life is hid with Christ in God (Col 3:1-3).

Paul writes to those who have been lifted into the heavenly places by the grace of God offered through Jesus Christ. But clearly, Paul is not applauding them for their decision. On the contrary, he is directing them to move beyond the grace offered them through faith. Concisely stated, Paul is commanding the Colossians to become in their experience what they already are through God's grace.

Paul's audience has been set free from the bondage of sin. By God's grace, they have become righteous, pure, and free from defect. God has exerted much effort to make this happen in their lives, but the time has come for the Colossians to exert some effort of their own. They must begin to speak, behave, and think as those who are raised up with Christ and who will one day appear with Him in glory.

> When Christ who is our life appears, then you also will appear with him in glory. Put to death therefore what is earthly in you: immorality, impurity, passion, evil desire, and covetousness, which is idolatry. On account of these the wrath of God is coming. In these you once walked, when you lived in them. But now put them all away: anger, wrath, malice, slander, and foul talk from your mouth. Do not lie to one another, seeing that you have put off the old nature with its practices and have put on the new nature, which is being renewed in knowledge after the image of its creator (Col 3:4-10).

Initially, two observations can be made concerning these verses, observations which reiterate conclusions already made. First of all, to accomplish something, Christians must often work in two different directions. This was observed in the discussion of the fourth beatitude concerning the need for believers to simultaneously mourn over sin and hunger for righteousness. Here in Colossians, we have approximately the same instruction.

Christians are to "seek the things above" by re-evaluating and re-adjusting the things around them. Said another way, the new nature is "put on" through ongoing communion with God (verse 10) and the old nature is gradually discarded as the Christian struggles to be free from certain behaviors and attitudes. An examination of these behaviors and attitudes leads to the second observation that can be made about these verses: if the earthly nature is to occupy less space within us, it will occur as we modify the way we interact with, and relate to, one other.

Paul's two lists each contain what are essentially five injunctions. And these mandates are satisfied, not by the will of God, but by the will of humankind. Grace provides only the opportunity for these behaviors and attitudes to be assimilated, not the behaviors and attitudes themselves. As we examine these, it will become increasingly clear that Christians are raised to newness of life that they might begin to live in a brand new manner.

"Put to death immorality"

"Immorality" comes first in Paul's list, retaining the same preeminence found in his list of the "works of the flesh" recorded in Galatians 5:19-21. From its primary position, it can be concluded that the sin carries a weight not shared by the others.

Primarily, the word, "immorality" refers to being involved with a prostitute, but the term carries a wider meaning in that it refers to extra-marital activity (Matt 5:32; 19:9). Concerning both, there is clear scriptural prohibition.

This teaching carries with it resounding clarity, but at the same time, it must be tempered with other scriptural portions which contain equal, if not greater lucidity.

> Early in the morning he came again to the temple; all the people came to him, and he sat down and taught them. The scribes and the Pharisees brought a woman who had been caught in adultery, and placing her in the midst they said to him, "Teacher, this woman has been caught in the act of

adultery. Now in the law Moses commanded us to stone such. What do you say about her?" This they said to test him, that they might have some charge to bring against him. Jesus bent down and wrote with his finger on the ground. And as they continued to ask him, he stood up and said to them, "Let him who is without sin among you be the first to throw a stone at her." And once more he bent down and wrote with his finger on the ground. But when they heard it, they went away, one by one, beginning with the eldest, and Jesus was left alone with the woman standing before him. Jesus looked up and said to her, "Woman, where are they? Has no one condemned you?" She said, "No one, Lord." And Jesus said, "Neither do I condemn you; go, and do not sin again" (John 8:2-11).

The scribes and the Pharisees effectively display a common tendency among many people, and that is to lift up the sins of others. And what is so completely reprehensible about such behavior is that it originates within those who are themselves sinful.

From Jesus Himself, we discover that such behavior is unacceptable even among those who are completely righteous in every respect. Jesus was such a person, and therefore had the legal right to stone the woman to her death. But, ironically, it was precisely because of Jesus' righteousness that the woman's life was spared and her soul forgiven. What can be concluded is that an inability to forgive comes from a sinful heart while a willingness to forgive springs from righteousness.

In their attempt to publicize the sin of another, the scribes and the Pharisees only succeed in condemning their own sinful behavior. The woman's accusers, in all of their self-righteousness, feel it necessary to leave the Master's presence. The woman, on the other hand, in all of her alleged sinfulness, remains with Him, completely absolved from her sins.

It is true that involvement in prostitution and extra-marital sexual activity is taught to be in direct opposition to the righteousness required for the kingdom of God (Matt 21:31; Lk 15:30). But what is also taught is that Jesus' invitation into the kingdom of God awakened penitence within prostitutes (Lk 7:50), and indeed brought them much more powerfully to repentance than it did the Pharisees who were supposedly those who personified moral correctness.

> [T]ruly I say to you, the tax collectors and the harlots go into the kingdom of God before you. For John came to you in the way of righteousness, and you did not believe him, but the tax collectors and the harlots believed him; and even when you saw it, you did not afterward repent and believe him (Matt 21:31-32).

"Put to death impurity"

Being "impure" is a pre-Christian state, that which is generally descriptive of a person not yet introduced to the cleansing only Jesus Christ provides. However, from Colossians 3, it is clear that those who accept Jesus Christ still struggle to release themselves completely from impurities. Although many different "acts" point to a state of "impurity," what Paul probably has in mind primarily are those impure acts related to ethical behavior. And clearly, the ethical behavior of Christians is to be beyond reproach.

Many Christians overlook the tremendous significance attached to the everyday treatment of other people. Clearly, it is the most telling indication of where a person is concerning spiritual development. But, at the same time, proper ethical behavior does not necessarily confirm the eradication of "impurity." If this were the case, then the inward transformation accomplished through Jesus Christ would be of secondary importance to the way in which people "carry" themselves.

It is interesting how some communities view the grace of God as being operational only in their particular circle, as though their distinctive approach to religion, with its accompanying methodologies, is the only manner in which God can be "properly" engaged. This "elitism" inevitably classifies other communities as those who practice a religion based upon works, the conclusion being twofold: (1) God's grace cannot possibly be in operation, and (2) the works performed by these other religious groups are without value because they do not spring from grace.

The arrogance is, at times, inconceivable. First of all, God's grace and while we are at it, God's Spirit, are both capable of working in ways far greater and with much greater diversity than any one person or any one group can even begin to imagine. And secondly, to belittle the "good works" of God's people as though they are without merit, is to deride the one thing for which all of God's people, regardless of denominational affiliation, should be striving with great diligence. Indeed, it is by their fruits that they shall be known.

"Impurity" lies resident in the immaterial portion of our being, and therefore, must be purged from within. It is a complete misnomer to conclude that purification is accomplished as a person, in a very mechanical manner, "learns" to remove evidence of impurity from the sight of others. But, at the same time, as the inner cleansing takes place, the outer person is transformed, and relationships are recast.

One of the effects of "putting to death" impurity is that a person becomes less pre-occupied with self. And as self-centeredness becomes less of a pre-occupation, behaviors completely incompatible with the newly created person also diminish.

For example, as a person becomes less self-centered, there is less of a tendency to be guarded and defensive, as though the next word or action of another person is going to be a personal attack or, at the very least, some form of disparagement. As self-centeredness fades, so does a person's tendency to feel as though mistreatment and injustice lie just around the corner.

When a person accepts Jesus Christ, some "impurities" fall immediately by the wayside. But there are always other "impurities" which are far more difficult to deal with. And these, of course, vary from person to person. Yes, even for Christians, there is the struggle with impurity. But, as long as the struggle remains, so too does the possibility that they will be eliminated.

> So then, brethren, we are debtors, not to the flesh, to live according to the flesh--for if you live according to the flesh you will die, but if by the Spirit you put to death the deeds of the body you will live (Rom 8:12-13).

"Put to death passion and evil desire"

The Greek word behind the word, "passion" is found only three times in the New Testament. In addition to Colossians 3, the word is found in Romans and 1 Thessalonians. Because the reference in Colossians is found in a list and therefore, has no context, only the other two passages will be quoted.

> Therefore God gave them up in the lusts of their hearts to impurity, to the dishonoring of their bodies among themselves, because they exchanged the truth about God for a lie and worshiped and served the creature rather than the Creator, who is blessed for ever! Amen. For this reason God gave them up to dishonorable *passions*. Their women exchanged natural relations for unnatural, and the men likewise gave up natural relations with women and were consumed with passion for one

another, men committing shameless acts with men and receiving in their own persons the due penalty for their error (Rom 1:24-27).

For this is the will of God, your sanctification: that you abstain from immorality; that each one of you know how to take a wife for himself in holiness and honor, not in the *passion* of lust like heathen who do not know God (1 Thess 4:3-5).

From these two portions of Scripture, it seems clear that "passion" has much to do with sexual activity displeasing to God. But the word, "passion" refers to more than sexual experience. Any overwhelming feeling which overtakes and overpowers, whether it be anger or lust or anything else, is that which we are to "put to death."

The point is that no part of ourselves must be allowed to control and dominate us. Every portion of our being must be brought under the authority of God, for God does not do well with rivalries. He will compete with no one or no thing.

One thing that must be understood about "passion" is that it exists within a person. It is not yet an act, but that which leads to it. Passion is many things. It is the uncontrollable jealousy that leads to murder; it is also the unmanageable craving that leads to sexual immorality. "Passion" is that which controls a person to the point where that person becomes a passive instrument of that feeling. It is that which overwhelms and overtakes.

Let us remember that "passion" goes beyond our feelings and our emotions. It cannot be simply defined as anger or sexual stimulation. These are natural and God-given, and when used properly, are quite acceptable and profitable. But when they are no longer manageable, no longer a controlled part of our lives, they are then a hindrance concerning our relationship with God; they must then be discarded.

While "passion" is the passive side of a vice, "evil desire" is the active side. While the former has more to do with the desire lying behind a particular act, the latter has more to do with the manifestation of the "passion" which, as we have seen, is a controlling force. Obviously, these kinds of actions are wholly incompatible with the life of a person who has been "raised up with Christ."

"Evil desire" displays an inability to be self-controlled, but more than this, it is an anxious self-seeking. It is the result of a self-centeredness that seizes the moment in whatever way necessary to satisfy whatever craving is present. It does not weigh the possible consequences and it does not consider the possible effect on others. Its singular purpose is to follow through on whatever impulse is at hand.

"Evil desire" is incapable of perceiving a situation through the eyes of another. More than one perspective simply does not exist. Much will be discussed concerning this later, but let it be said for now that far too many people are incapable of viewing circumstances through any perspective but their own. And this narrow-mindedness is responsible, in varying measures, for many, if not all of the attitudes and behaviors which are to be removed from the lives of those professing faith in Jesus Christ.

In summary, emotional capacity is God-given. Even those feelings routinely categorized as "unfavorable," are not necessarily ungodly. However, if they begin to master us, leaving us helpless to control them, they then become incompatible with our new nature. If they become unmanageable to the point where they are manifested in behavior, we have succeeded in epitomizing that which defines sinful activity: a self-directed act which does not weigh consequences or take into account the possible effects on any other person; action devoid of purpose, behavior without consideration of conscience.

"Put to death covetousness"

There is an emphasis placed upon the danger of "covetousness" that is not evidenced in the sins preceding it. And the emphasis is created as "covetousness" is linked closely with "idolatry": "Put to death . . . *and covetousness, which is idolatry*" (Col 3:5).

To "covet" means to "desire more." It has much to do with, but is not limited to, "greed" and "insatiableness." As a matter of fact, in the strict sense of the word, a person "covets" when there is striving for *any* earthly provision, regardless of its size or utilitarian value.

This definition offers some explanation as to why "covetousness" is spoken in the same breath as "idolatry." Generally speaking, if a person is not seeking God, that person is seeking those things which are not of God. And a striving for that which is not God-related is idolatry.

Every person is driven by something, or maybe more appropriately, *to* something. It may be another person or another possession or another level of "power," however "power" might be defined. But whatever the ambition, there is always someone or something that brings meaning and purpose to existence. When there are no longer any goals, there is, very simply, no longer any need, or desire, to exist. Therefore, for most people, if one goal is no longer driving them, then, inevitably, another goal or ambition takes its place.

In Paul's letter to the Colossians, he encourages his readers to take their minds off earthly things and concentrate exclusively on the things of God. In other words, the apostle Paul teaches people to be driven by something other than the things of the earth and the need for self-fulfillment that so often accompanies it.

The prophet Micah speaks words to the people of his day which could just as easily be spoken to the people of our society.

> Woe to those who devise wickedness and work evil upon their beds! When the morning dawns, they perform it, because it is in the power of their hand. They covet fields, and seize them; and houses, and take them away; they oppress a man and his house, a man and his inheritance. Therefore thus says the LORD: Behold, against this family I am devising evil, from which you cannot remove your necks; and you shall not talk haughtily, for it will be an evil time. In that day they shall take up a taunt song against you, and wail with bitter lamentation, and say, "We are utterly ruined; he changes the portion of my people; how he removes it from me! Among our captors he divides our fields." Therefore you will have none to cast the line by lot in the assembly of the LORD (Mic 2:1-5).

Micah's words were directed to those in positions of authority and therefore, to those who had the ability to accomplish what is for many only a desire. But, we must remember, that whether or not tangible results are associated with covetous desires, the sin of covetousness remains.

"Covetousness" brings us back to selfishness. The one who is selfish is not concerned about God or the helpless or the weak. On the contrary, the person who is selfish is concerned primarily with receiving things himself. And interestingly enough, as this person possesses the various objects of his covetous desire, that person begins to believe that he has received exactly what is deserved. And furthermore, the various possessions are thought to be part of the manifest blessings of God.

An insidious web is created as people, snared by their own self-centeredness, conclude that the activity of God is being exercised primarily on their behalf, as though they are somehow more favored than others. As long as personal wants and desires are fulfilled, there is no difficulty. But as soon as earthly needs are no longer met, there are at least two possible complications that result: (1) the conclusion that God is displeased with the person, and (2) God does not really care after all.

An Appropriate Attitude

There is an attitude, a position if you will, concerning God and self, that we would all do well to cultivate. And it is an attitude found in the recorded words of the 90th psalmist. As we give this psalm a brief examination, it becomes clear that the psalmist is driven by something other than the need for power and possessions. He is driven instead by the need to bring his existence a higher, more noble meaning, one that is derived from, therefore reflective of, his association with God.

What assists the psalmist tremendously is the comprehension he has of his own overall significance relative to that of God's. In comparison, the psalmist's significance is non-existent.

> Before the mountains were brought forth, or ever thou hadst formed the earth and the world, from everlasting to everlasting thou art God. Thou turnest man back to the dust, and sayest, "Turn back, O children of men!" For a thousand years in thy sight are but as yesterday when it is past, or as a watch in the night. Thou dost sweep men away; they are like a dream, like grass which is renewed in the morning: in the morning it flourishes and is renewed; in the evening it fades and withers (Ps 90:2-6).

God's time places our own in perspective. While He is from everlasting to everlasting, we, in comparison, are nothing more than grass which flourishes in the morning, and fades towards evening.

What is implicit in these verses is that any credit for "flourishing" in this world must be given to God. Regardless of what people believe concerning themselves, they are, in and of themselves, nothing. If there is to be real purpose and meaning to one's existence, then that existence must be made subject to the Creator. If life is to realize its "God-intended" significance, then everything associated with life, including its goals and intentions, must be filtered through the existence of God. Apart from this filtering process, there is no hope for life to possess true meaning or to contain any measure of ultimate value. For these to exist, there must be God's control, not our own.

As the psalmist pondered his own existence, he concluded there to be a certain futility associated with it. Futhermore, he concluded it was God's desire for him to feel as though life was without meaning.

In the psalmist's mind, it was good that life was short, because with this realization came the desire to fill every day with significance. The realization of futility compelled the psalmist to search for that which gave his life purpose. And for the psalmist, that search led him into the very presence of God.

At first, verses 7-12 seem out of place. After six verses of solemn reflection on the existence of God and man, suddenly, the psalmist makes reference to the way in which God's wrath and anger invade the lives of His people.

> For we are consumed by thy anger; by thy wrath we are overwhelmed. Thou hast set our iniquities before thee, our secret sins in the light of thy countenance. For all our days pass away under thy wrath, our years come to an end like a sigh. The years of our life are threescore and ten, or even by reason of strength fourscore; yet their span is but toil and trouble; they are soon gone, and we fly away. Who considers the

power of thy anger, and thy wrath according to the fear of thee? (Ps 90:7-11)

The psalmist still speaks of days being limited, but now he does so in the context of how God judges people for their sins. The psalmist speaks of the wrath and the anger, even the fury of the Lord, and at first, the words don't seem to flow from the words preceding them. But when we read verse 12, we see what point the psalmist is making, for he says, "So teach us to number our days that we may get a heart of wisdom" (Ps 90:12).

People have approximately seventy years to do something with their lives. At the end of that time, they stand before God and give account of what they have done. The psalmist reminds us that our time on earth is on the same continuum as our time of giving account before God. Life leads to death just as a time for proving ourselves leads to an ascription of value concerning that time, value which is ascribed by God and no other.

The fact that we will one day stand before God and give an accounting of what we have done and for that matter, what we have not done, instills a certain amount of apprehension concerning that day. And this apprehension prompts a certain amount of reflection concerning the days in which we presently live. Clearly, this is the psalmist's intention, that his audience might search for meaning to their existence as he himself did. And furthermore, that their search would carry them to the conclusion that real meaning and purpose came only as life was lived in accordance with the plan of God.

It is an understanding of self relative to a comprehension of God that formulates much of the psalmist's attitude. And this attitude is poignantly expressed in a series of prayers found at the end of the psalm. The first is "So teach us to number our days that we may get a heart of wisdom" (Ps 90:12).

This simple prayer requests that life be seen, not only as a time that is short, but as a time that is allotted. In other words, it is a prayer for perspective, one that allows us to see, not only that life will one day end, but that the time available has been granted by God as a great gift.

While some lament the brevity of life, the proper response can only be one of gratitude. The time given by God is filled with possibility and opportunity. Therefore, the gift of life must not be approached with lamentation, for it is an unfathomable and inexhaustible reality.

In verse 14, the psalmist prays, "Satisfy us in the morning with thy steadfast love, that we may rejoice and be glad all our days." This prayer reveals the psalmist's belief that life is meant to have a quality associated with it, a quality which is born only in the heart of God.

Life is not meant to be filled with routine and convention. Instead, life is to be filled, even driven, by the gift of God's steadfast love. Only then does life become something other than predictable and uneventful. Only then do the seventy years of life have a meaningful, timeless quality.

The prayer in verse 15 expresses an attitude that is found in very few people. "Lord, make us glad as many days as you have afflicted us, and as many years as we have seen evil." Here, the psalmist reminds us that even though our life can be filled with the steadfast love of the Lord, there is also associated with it a degree of pain and toil.

The difficulty of life persists, even with the presence of God, but the psalmist's prayer is not that the pain and hardship be erased, that the struggle might somehow be eliminated. Instead, there is a request for as many days of happiness as there are days of sadness. In other words, the psalmist does not expect to live a trouble-free existence. For him, it is not even necessary.

His association with God is undoubtedly the reason, for it is only an absence of God that demands an uncomplicated, unencumbered life.

It is only a life devoid of God's presence that cries out for an absence of trial and difficulty. With God, such unrealistic expectations are unnecessary.

How is it so many people miss the clear message associated with scriptural truths found in the recorded stories of men like Job and Jeremiah? These were righteous men deeply concerned about their relationships with God. Clearly, this relationship was what drove both of them, but their convictions and their devotion did not keep them from the trials of life. On the contrary, it was their association with God that introduced them to a good portion of it.

In light of this, how can people question someone's faith in God simply because of that person's experience with hindrances and set-backs? Those who question the faith of others for these reasons succeed in proving their ignorance concerning God and the ways in which God's will intersects with the lives of His people. Such questions succeed in reducing both God and human life to that which is ridiculously predictable, even absurd.

> As he passed by, he saw a man blind from his birth. And his disciples asked him, "Rabbi, who sinned, this man or his parents, that he was born blind?" Jesus answered, "It was not that this man sinned, or his parents, but that the works of God might be made manifest in him" (John 9:1-3).

The 16th verse records another prayer, "Lord let your work be manifest to your servants and your glorious power to their children." This prayer speaks to the multitude of people who, for whatever reason, are able to see only the evil of life, with its many inconsistencies and absurdities.

While the wonder of God and the many miracles of God are everywhere on a daily basis, many people, even those who are

Christians, focus primarily upon that which is not of God. For some reason, it is easier for many to find the flaws, to highlight the imperfections, to discuss the evil. While God's presence effectively counteracts all of this, His work often remains unspoken and therefore, unpraised.

We all need to see more than the absurdities and the potential entanglements. While the sadness and the pain exist, there is so much more. "Lord, Let thy work be manifest to thy servants, and thy glorious power to their children."

The final prayer is that we may be confirmed in our own work and calling, that in some way God will make secure what we do, that He will give our work a place. "Let the favor of the Lord our God be upon us, and establish thou the work of our hands upon us, yea, the work of our hands establish thou it" (Ps 90:17).

This is not a prayer for fame and greatness. It is not even a prayer that we might see the fulfillment, or the consequence, or the outcome of our work. Instead, it is a prayer that our work might be established, that God may bring whatever work we do into being and give it an enduring value.

As we examine these prayers found in Psalm 90, it becomes clear that the psalmist is concerned about his life, but in a very unselfish manner. He desires meaning for his life, but meaning that is found only as he works to accomplish God's will, not his own. His attitude clearly points to a person who has transcended covetous thought.

We would do well to remember that when a person loses sight of God, that person is at the mercy of all other things. Because people are always driven by something and toward something, God must be involved in the process, or covetousness will come to take God's place.

In the Ten Commandments, there is no key phrase repeated more than, "Thou shall not covet." The decision to be content in our present state is not only a command of God, but what rational analysis concludes to be absolutely necessary if life is to continue.

Each person must decide individually what is to grow. Will it be giving or receiving, income or outlay, covetousness or contentment? And while we are at it, who is it we have placed in charge of our futures? Do we arrogantly continue to plot our own course, or have we given God His rightful place? Where are our minds? Have we put to death the things of this earth, or do we still keep a foot or two in that from which we have been redeemed?

Selfish greed cannot guarantee the future, only misbuild it. But the person whose mind and heart are stayed upon the power and presence of God is one whose future has already been determined. This person need not go through his days fretting over the tomorrows, for they have already been numbered in the infinitesimal mind of God. And covetousness works against, even destroys that which has been ordained.

Paul offers this list of five sins in Colossians 3 and then comments, "On account of these the wrath of God is coming" (Col 3:6). While some translations allow the reader to assume it to be a future wrath of which Paul speaks, the original language clearly indicates present tense. In other words, unlike the future judgment spoken by the 90th psalmist, the apostle Paul refers to the anger of God which comes as a direct consequence of the sin, revealed at a time immediately following the sin. Therefore, judgment is not only a future event but a present reality.

People bring many consequences of sin upon themselves. Concerning this, there can be no question. In a very real sense, sinful people experience the outworking of their own immorality. But in another very real sense, God does not stand as one who simply views the various consequences, but as one directly involved with their formulation.

For the wrath of God is revealed from heaven against all ungodliness and wickedness of men who by their wickedness suppress the truth . . . although they knew God they did not honor him as God or give thanks to him, but they became futile in their thinking and their senseless minds were darkened . . . Therefore God gave them up in the lusts of their hearts to impurity, to the dishonoring of their bodies among themselves . . . For this reason God gave them up to dishonorable passions . . . And since they did not see fit to acknowledge God, God gave them up to a base mind and to improper conduct (Rom 1:18-28).

According to this list of sins in Colossians 3, God's wrath comes to those who do not allow their redemption to transform the relationships they have with one another. The apostle Paul teaches that these sins must cease, that they must be "put to death."

Removing The Old

From this list, the apostle moves almost immediately to another list of sins that must be "laid aside" by those who have been changed by God's grace. And once again, the transformation has everything to do with the way God's people treat one another. But there is a noticeable change in emphasis.

In the first list, the apostle highlighted sins which result from mismanagement of sensuality. In the second list, Paul's emphasis is on sins which result from the misuse of the tongue.

"Lay aside anger"

Although God's anger exists alongside His love without confusion, this is not the case, scripturally speaking, with people. Concerning the people of God, love and anger are mutually exclusive.

Only in two instances does the New Testament estimate human anger in a way that is something other than clearly negative (Rom 10:19; 2 Cor 7:11). What is much more common is an appraisal of anger that is anything but positive.

Outbursts of anger are never pleasant, and it is not surprising that the Bible instructs God's people to lay aside such an emotion. But anger does contain a constructive element, one that is not always easy to discover, but an element for which every mature Christian must search.

When a person becomes angry, the immediate tendency is to respond in a similar fashion. It is a natural (earthly) way for people to protect themselves. But it is precisely this "natural" response that Christians must work to transform, for such a reaction only succeeds in creating an even more unstable situation and therefore, one that is less manageable.

Those who have been redeemed through Jesus Christ are expected to control anger. Obviously, this means they are expected to control their own anger, but more than this, they are expected to control the anger of others in a way that is beneficial and productive.

This is possible only as we begin to view another person's anger as an opportunity to learn and offer support. This is never accomplished as we see their anger and respond to it with our own. Instead, a person's anger must be seen as an indication of unresolved difficulty. Only then are we able to focus our attention behind the anger and have any chance of discerning the root cause of the outburst.

As we saw in the beatitudes, followers of Christ are expected to be peacemakers. This means that we control our own anger, even if provoked. It also means we attempt to control the anger of others by responding to it constructively.

Obviously, it is not always easy to pinpoint the root cause of a person's anger, for outbursts may occur at times which have absolutely nothing to do with the actual problem. People will often times vent their frustrations in ways that are not only unproductive, but at times that offer little or no clue as to the real difficulty.

Because anger is a very complex emotion, we must learn to do at least two things as those who have been redeemed by Jesus Christ: (1) look beyond a person's anger in an attempt to discern the difficulty which lies behind it, and (2) not take outbursts personally and respond with anger ourselves.

Anger MUST be controlled by those who have accepted Christ, for outbursts of anger (1) destroy Christian harmony, (2) work against the building of righteousness, and (3) offer extremely poor testimony to those who are considering a Christian walk. Anger MUST be controlled.

"Lay aside wrath"

Although many reference books point to a subtle distinction between "anger" and "wrath," there is more than subtlety that separates them. In Romans 2:8, Ephesians 4:31 and Colossians 3:8, these words occur next to one another, not because they are synonymns but because they make reference to two separate emotions. And according to Paul, BOTH of these emotions must be laid aside.

Surely, there are many notable differences between "anger" and "wrath," but what is perhaps the most significant is best understood by an examination of two issues associated with them: (1) the amount of self-control involved, and (2) the existence, or lack thereof, of anticipated result or culmination.

With "anger," there is little or no control, deliberacy, or anticipation of closure. On the contrary, it is, more than anything else, a "venting." As previously discussed, "anger" is something that can rise quickly, without warning or any real provocation. The moment at hand is not necessarily related to the "anger" directly, only that which, for whatever reason, taps a nerve and prompts a response. Generally speaking, "anger" is without productivity. "Wrath," on the other hand, is very different.

Most of the references to "wrath" in the New Testament provide little or no context. Therefore, they offer little or no illumination concerning meaning. But this changes in the book of Revelation. In this book, there are several references to divine wrath, but perhaps none offer as much definitional insight as the following verse:

> Then I saw another portent in heaven, great and wonderful, seven angels with seven plagues, which are the last, for with them the *wrath* of God is ended (Rev 15:1).

In the book of Revelation, "wrath" is only used in reference to God. This by itself demonstrates an "emotion" that has definite purpose, therefore, a terminal quality. In other words, God is not angrily out of control, but deliberate and thought-filled concerning His actions. They are designed to produce certain results.

One last distinction to be made between "anger" and "wrath" has to do with the focus of the two emotions. With "anger," there are either past or present circumstances which prompt its manifestation. But with "wrath," while there are certainly past events which provoke its existence, its focus is primarily forward. "Wrath" is itself, predetermined, and directed towards accomplishment. It is calculated and studied, not momentary, careless and inadvertent.

While Scriptures are very comfortable with God exhibiting "wrath," the Bible is not at all tolerant of people being in possession of it. Concerning God and His creation, there are vast differences in capacities, capabilities and intellectual competence. One has a world view; the other has an extremely narrow, selfish perspective. One is proficient at perceiving various consequences; the other is mostly cognizant of his immediate needs.

Even Christians are incapable of a proper and appropriate distribution of "wrath." They are called upon to "lay it aside." And this is something of which Christians should be appreciative. With wrath, there is too much room for error and too much responsibility associated with it. Decidedly, it is best left in the hands of God.

"Lay aside malice"

"Malice" is variously translated as "trouble," "evil," "unrighteousness," and "wickedness." The term is a general one ranging from "trouble" in Matthew's gospel to a decidedly culpable attitude of wickedness in Acts 8.

> But seek first his kingdom and his righteousness, and all these things shall be yours as well. Therefore do not be anxious about tomorrow, for tomorrow will be anxious for itself. Let the day's own *trouble* be sufficient for the day (Matt 6:33-34).

> Now when Simon saw that the Spirit was given through the laying on of the apostles' hands, he offered them money, saying, "Give me also this power, that any one on whom I lay my hands may receive the Holy Spirit." But Peter said to him, "Your silver perish with you, because you thought you could obtain the gift of God with money! You have neither part nor lot in this matter, for your heart is not right before God. Repent therefore of this *wickedness* of yours, and pray to the Lord that, if possible, the intent of your heart may be forgiven you (Acts 8:18-22).

From these two examples, we see that the word, "malice," encompasses a large semantic field. Its definition lies in a range from that which has no moral value to behavior whose moral value is great. But in relation to Colossians, the context of the larger list of which "malice" is a part, suggests that its meaning has to do with verbal activity disruptive of harmonious relationships. Paul's letter to the Ephesians offers clarification.

> Let no evil talk come out of your mouths, but only such as is good for edifying, as fits the occasion, that it may impart grace to those who hear. And do not grieve the Holy Spirit of God, in whom you were sealed for the day of redemption. Let all bitterness and wrath and anger and clamor and slander be put away from you, with all *malice*, and be kind to one another, tenderhearted, forgiving one another, as God in Christ forgave you (Eph 4:29-32).

Clearly, the apostle's list, of which "malice" is a part, comprises those things related to human speech. And the admonition, much like that found in Colossians, is for the Christian to "put these things away."

What must not be overlooked is that Paul's instructions related to human relationships have as part of their blend, a warning against the grieving of the Holy Spirit. In other words, Paul speaks of the disruption of human relationships in the same breath as he speaks of an interruption of one's association with God, indicating their intimate relationship. And he does so by speaking primarily of the way we relate to one another with words.

> Put off your old nature which belongs to your former manner of life and is corrupt through deceitful lusts, and be renewed in the spirit of your minds, and put on the new nature, created

after the likeness of God in true righteousness and holiness. Therefore, putting away falsehood, let every one speak the truth with his neighbor, for we are members one of another (Eph 4:22-25).

Much more will be said about the use and misuse of the tongue. It is truly that which "no human being can tame--a restless evil, full of deadly poison" (James 3:8). And that leads us to the next "sin" in Paul's list.

"Lay aside slander"

Much of the overall argument presented thus far involves the need for a person's association with God to manifest itself in everyday relationships. In other words, as I have said before, what people have become by God's grace, they must now become in their actions. An examination of the word, "slander" offers even more evidence regarding the validity of this claim.

The word from which "slander" is translated is more often rendered, "blasphemy" in the New Testament. And certainly, this rendering is preferred when there is reference to some kind of "speech against God." "Blasphemy" can be directed immediately against God (Rev 13:6; 16:11, 21), against the name of God (Rom 2:24; 1 Tim 6:1), against the word of God (Tit 2:5), and against the bearer of the revelation in the law (Acts 6:11). But the word from which "blasphemy" is derived can also be used to denote slanderous or abusive speaking against one another, as is the case in Colossians. Then, the word is better translated, "slander."

In Paul's first epistle to the church at Corinth, he speaks repeatedly of the need for Christian conduct to manifest the characteristics of God, teaching that God is glorified as Christians seek the welfare of one another.

The apostle was undoubtedly besieged by innumerable questions related to Christian conduct. And naturally, it was impossible for him to address them all individually. Instead, he offered some general principles related to Christian behavior, leaving the application of these principles to the Corinthians.

According to Paul, a believer's conduct (1) should be beneficial (1 Cor 6:12), (2) should not be enslaving (1 Cor 6:12), (3) should not hinder the spiritual growth of a brother (1 Cor 8:13), and (4) should be edifying (1 Cor 10:23).

There is definitely something to be gained by leaving the specific application of general guidelines to the individual. Only by wrestling with their application does a person begin to actually understand and incorporate their true meaning and purpose.

If absolute rules were to be handed down for everyone to follow, people would develop the ability to follow directions. What would be the point of bringing all questions to some higher source and simply receiving the direction? The only thing accomplished would be the manufacturing of Christian drones, those who operate without real understanding and without conviction of their own. Is this what God would have His people become? I think not.

It is important to observe that the same word for "abusive speech" is used in reference to both God and people. Not only do we again see how a person's relationship with God is almost interchangeable with relationships that person has with others, but we see the great deal of importance God places upon the way we speak to one another. As God is displeased with "blasphemous" language directed toward Him, so is He displeased with the "slanderous" language that is all too often directed toward one another.

There is no challenge in finding something negative, then making comment concerning it. The errors and weaknesses of people are on abundant display every day. While there are some people seemingly incapable of discovering that which is admirable or excellent, the real difficulty for most lies in the willingness to make simple comment concerning such things. It is as though people believe their own selves will be diminished if another is exalted.

"Slander" is a completely culpable sin with which far too many people have become far too comfortable. It is disturbing that such failing has found such a large degree of acceptance. And it would be well for people to remember the words of Jesus recorded by Luke.

> Nothing is covered up that will not be revealed, or hidden that will not be known. Whatever you have said in the dark shall be heard in the light, and what you have whispered in private rooms shall be proclaimed upon the housetops. I tell you, my friends, do not fear those who kill the body, and after that have no more that they can do. But I will warn you whom to fear: fear him who, after he has killed, has power to cast into hell; yes, I tell you, fear him! (Lk 12:2-5)

"Lay aside foul talk"

People cannot help but perceive life from within their own realm of certainty. This means that, among other things, people are predetermined in their thoughts and convictions concerning the expectations of God's Word. Whether people realize it or not, much of what they glean from Scriptures is largely determined before the divine wisdom is even in hand. And no where is this more clearly illustrated than in the passages related to the words which proceed from our mouths.

The command in Colossians to lay aside "foul talk" is very straightforward. And in the same manner Paul brought emphasis to the admonition concerning "covetousness," he does so with "foul talk" by adding words concerning it: ". . . and foul talk *from your mouth*."

Obviously, "from your mouth" is an unnecessary addendum for "foul talk" can only come from a person's mouth. But Paul's desire is not to state the obvious, but to underscore the significance of "foul talk" relative to the other words in his list.

"Foul talk" is best understood broadly as language which is not reflective of God. In other words, any utterance which is not representative of God Himself is absolutely prohibited. "Foul talk" is that which is shameful, emanating from the base portion of our structure. It is that which issues from our former selves which were supposedly put to death by the grace of God through His Son Jesus Christ. "Foul talk" encompasses any language that is obscene, abusive or in any other way, a departure from the divine nature placed within us that is always supportive, always encouraging, and always uplifting.

As direct and straightforward as scriptural passages are concerning the call for God's people to cease from their ungodly use of the tongue, people continue to bemoan all that is "not" rather than celebrate what "is." Even though biblical mandates abound, even so-called believers find it much easier to belittle the efforts of others rather than to commend them for their struggle. Harsh, bitter words are offered instead of encouragement. Mouths invalidate the efforts, even the very existence of God's people. And sarcastic tones and cynical attitudes are much more the rule than they are the exception.

People are desensitized to the destructive nature of such language. Not only is it commonplace, but it is accepted as a part of everyday conversation. Part of the problem comes from the fact that people do not think it possible to cease from such habits. As a result, they overlook the scriptural teaching concerning it, allowing their predeterminations to convince them that cessation is impossible. Consequently, the ungodly language continues.

Admittedly, old habits associated with the tongue die with great difficulty. But what must be remembered is that scriptural mandates concerning these habits are some of the most plain and most repeated.

In all of our Christian endeavors, we must recognize that barriers once insurmountable are now very much absent. The same rules no longer apply as limitations formerly established are now simply curtains to be pushed through. Earthly restrictions encompassing our former selves have been transformed into very real possibilities.

Concerning "foul talk," patterns can be transformed. Indeed, they MUST be transformed if we are to satisfy the very clear, straightforward direction of God.

> Do not lie to one another, seeing that you have put off the old nature with its practices and have put on the new nature, which is being renewed in knowlege after the image of its creator. Here there cannot be Greek and Jew, circumcised and uncircumcised, barbarian, Scythian, slave, free man, but Christ is all, and in all. Put on then, as God's chosen ones, holy and beloved, compassion, kindness, lowliness, meekness, and patience, forbearing one another and, if one has a complaint against another, forgiving each other; as the Lord has forgiven you, so you also must forgive. And above all these put on love, which binds everything together in perfect harmony. And let the peace of Christ rule in your hearts, to which indeed you were called in the one body. And be thankful. Let the word of Christ dwell in you richly, as you teach and admonish one another in all wisdom, and as you sing psalms and hymns and spiritual songs with thankfulness in your hearts to God. *And whatever you do, in word or deed, do everything in the name of the Lord Jesus,* giving thanks to God the Father through him (Col 3:9-17).

Clearly, every single word that proceeds from our mouths is to be representative of the character of God given to us through the work of Jesus Christ. It is a difficult transformation but one that is available to all who open their minds and hearts to the possibility.

Goals and visions disappear
Romantic notions fade
Souls are cast, then find their place
Where irony is laid

Somber grays predominate
While sounds become less clear
Horizons fade, then find their place
In crags and chasms near

Darkness leads to summits lost
As whispers come along
Heights are razed, then find their place
When angels sing their song

Silent cries are heard by few
Angelic spirits pray
Songs are sent, then find their place
Lost souls now find their way
P. L. Engstrom

CHAPTER THREE
The Outward Reformation

If there is a purgatorial existence for those who falter in their efforts to be the people God would have them be, it is an experience to be had in this physical realm. Scripture repeatedly demonstrates the judgment of God to be that which results from certain behavior. At times, this behavior naturally shapes the consequences which follow. At other times, there is an active divine component.

Concerning the judgment of God, at least three things can be said: (1) it is most often the result of our own behavior, (2) it is routinely experienced in this physical realm, and (3) its presentation as well as its parameters are defined by the behavior from which it proceeds. With a certainty, people bring upon themselves, not only "judgment," but its circumscription. And they do so by ignoring divine determinations issued for their own protection and benefit.

Hypocrisy Brings Disaster

It is most interesting that human nature is, and always has been, resolutely determined to bring hardship and difficulty upon itself. As a matter of fact, the Bible's introductory message communicates the human disposition towards disobedience and deceit.

Adam and Eve's Hypocrisy

There are two points made by the opening chapters of Genesis that could not have been expressed with any greater clarity: (1) God goes to great effort to provide humankind with absolutely everything necessary to live a trouble-free existence, and (2) Adam and Eve are unable to observe the only restriction given them. Concerning this single restraint, God's instructions were very straightforward.

> And the LORD God commanded the man, saying, "You may eat of every tree of the garden; but of the tree of the knowledge of good and evil you shall not eat, for in the day that you eat of it you shall die" (Gen 2:16-17).

In the next chapter, when Adam and Eve are confronted for the first time with the possibility of disobeying this single commandment, both falter.

> So when the woman saw that the tree was good for food, and that it was a delight to the eyes, and that the tree was to be desired to make one wise, she took of its fruit and ate; and she also gave some to her husband, and he ate. Then the eyes of both were opened, and they knew that they were naked; and they sewed fig leaves together and made themselves aprons (Gen 3:6-7).

Adam and Eve were given opportunity to act inappropriately, and they did. Interestingly enough, one resulting effect was they lost the complete trust and comfort they originally had with one another. Prior to their act of disobedience, nakedness before one another was not a problem. It was not even an issue. Only after they realized the "sinful" potential that lay resident within them were they no longer able to enjoy complete ease and relaxation with one another. "Sinful" potential was seen within one another, but also within themselves. As a result, they could no longer portray themselves to the other as they really were, for within them, lay that which needed to be covered.

A similar discomfort resulted where their relationship with God was concerned.

> And they heard the sound of the LORD God walking in the garden in the cool of the day, and the man and his wife hid themselves from the presence of the LORD God among the trees of the garden. But the LORD God called to the man, and said to him, "Where are you?" And he said, "I heard the sound of thee in the garden, and I was afraid, because I was naked; and I hid myself" (Gen 3:8-10).

And there were more relationships affected by the "sin" of Adam and Eve, one being that relationship between humankind and the serpent.

> Then the LORD God said to the woman, "What is this that you have done?" The woman said, "The serpent beguiled me, and I ate." The LORD God said to the serpent, "Because you have done this, cursed are you above all cattle, and above all wild animals; upon your belly you shall go, and dust you shall eat all the days of your life. I will put enmity between you and the woman, and between your seed and her seed; he shall bruise your head, and you shall bruise his heel (Gen 3:13-15).

"Enmity" or "hostility" did not exist between the serpent and humankind prior to Adam and Eve's act of disobedience. It was only after disobedience that Eve's cordial relationship with the serpent was altered, to the point where the serpent's very appearance was transformed.

Three more relationships were affected as a result of Adam and Eve's disobedience, two of which are expressed in the following passage.

> To the woman he said, "I will greatly multiply your pain in childbearing; in pain you shall bring forth children, yet your desire shall be for your husband, and he shall rule over you" (Gen 3:16).

As Eve was the representative of women in all generations, it was not just the relationship between her and her offspring that was affected; all women and their children have been affected through Eve's disobedience. And even though the words make reference specifically to the pain of childbirth, what is probably meant is the general struggle women have throughout the rearing of their children. Without original disobedience, it is probably safe to assume that there would be no sibling rivalry or teenage rebellion.

The language of Genesis also makes clear the subordination of women to men. There are many explanations concerning the "rule" men were given over women, ranging from natural physical strength to the Scriptures containing language and ideas reflective of a patriarachal system. But one thing that is clear is the relational change occuring as the direct result of disobedience. Prior to the act that "defiled," there was complete, unequivocal equality between Adam and Eve. Whatever the inequity that came into effect after the "fall," it was not a condition of "pre-fall" humanity. In other words, it was not part of God's original intention. And neither was the last relational change found in the following passage.

> And to Adam he said, "Because you have listened to the voice of your wife, and have eaten of the tree of which I commanded you, `You shall not eat of it,' cursed is the ground because of you; in toil you shall eat of it all the days of your life; thorns and thistles it shall bring forth to you; and you shall eat the plants of the field. In the sweat of your face you shall eat bread till you return to the ground, for out of it you were taken; you are dust, and to dust you shall return (Gen 3:17-19).

Adam, and for that matter, all men, were to struggle with the land in a way not originally intended by God. Throughout the Old Testament, there is a very close relationship among God, the people and the land. When the people of God are obedient, land is not only in abundance, but it is fruitful. When the people's relationship with God suffers, so also does the people's relationship with the land. There are famines, enemy incursions and deportations. The book of Exodus provides what is perhaps the most excellent study concerning the relationship that exists among God, the people and the land.

It is significant that the Genesis account of the emergence of "sinfulness" is presented by repeated references to outward appearances. Clearly, outward appearances are affected when internal purity is altered. As we have seen, (1) Adam and Eve become self-conscious of their appearance before one another, (2) before God, Adam and Eve find it necessary to hide themselves, (3) the serpent's appearance, even his very structure, is altered entirely, becoming a creature he was not previously, and (4) it is possible that men became more muscular, thus also undergoing physical transformation.

Adam and Eve were indeed representatives of people today. Amazingly, people have knowledge concerning behavior that is inappropriate, along with an understanding of the consequences of such actions, yet, people commit the acts anyway.

Like Adam and Eve, people behave inappropriately, then change their behavior in an attempt to cover it. In other words, people hide their "transgressions" by becoming something on the outside they are not on the inside.

This was precisely Jeremiah's point as he proclaimed God's Word to the temple-worshippers. These worshippers were very practiced when it came to standing in the right place, at the right time, saying the right words. But their activity away from the temple did not coincide with their demeanor while participating in worship services. Jeremiah's words to these people demonstrate that appearances can indeed be very deceiving. Naturally, he called upon them to become inwardly what they already projected outwardly.

There is nothing more damaging to a person's relationship with God, his friends and even himself, than when activity and behavior must be "covered." This is hypocrisy and it is the most pervasive, most damaging "sin" of them all.

Jesus and Hypocrisy

In Luke's gospel, we read of Jesus standing before thousands who had gathered to hear Him speak. In fact, there were so many that "they trod upon one another" (Lk 12:1).

Luke first tells of a marvelous opportunity Jesus had to reach an extremely large audience with His message. After revealing a scene too good to be imagined, the gospel writer, to the readers' surprise, then tells how Jesus turned away from them.

> In the meantime, when so many thousands of the multitude had gathered together that they trod upon one another, *he began to say to his disciples first,* "Beware of the leaven of the Pharisees, which is hypocrisy" (Lk 12:1).

Luke successfully communicates the importance of Jesus' words to the disciples by showing Jesus' willingness to delay an opportunity to speak to the "uninitiated." Presumably, it was more meaningful for the disciples to hear the message Jesus had for them than it was for the multitudes to receive their message.

At first, it may be difficult to understand how the teaching on hypocrisy could be so important. Certainly, it contained a warning to the disciples concerning the deceitful ways of the Pharisees. But more significantly, it was a personal word offered to the disciples concerning the incorporation of its message into their own lives.

Let us not be surprised that the disciples, like the people of our day, need to be warned concerning hypocrisy. There are far too many who claim to be Christians, but who, in reality, are putting on nothing more than a very effective display. There are many so-called Christians who are quite practiced at the art of deception and pretense. They know which words to speak and which activities to participated in, but when it comes right down to it, their life is largely a created facade. And though many are hurt as a result, no one person suffers more than the one involved in the deception; after a while, not even that person is able to distinguish between that which is real and that which is not.

We saw what happened to Adam and Eve as the result of their "hypocrisy." Becoming uncomfortable and hesitant, their trust in others and their confidence in themselves decreased. As a result, relationships were affected.

The spiritual and physical well-being of people would be greatly improved if there was not the constant expenditure of energy necessary to conceal that of which they are ashamed and to give the appearance of being someone they are not. God never intended His people to participate in such exercises. On the contrary, God designed His people to be a projection of their true selves. He intended there to be no hidden agendas, no concealed meanings, and no duplicity. Simply said, outward appearances are expected to be in harmony with the inner self.

Judas and Hypocrisy

Look at Judas for example. He reclined with Jesus and the other disciples at the passover table, doing his best to camouflage a plot in which he was involved to betray Jesus. However, Jesus knew of his deceit and commented,

> He who has dipped his hand in the dish with me, will betray me. The Son of man goes as it is written of him, but woe to that man by whom the Son of man is betrayed! It would have been better for that man if he had not been born (Matt 26:23-24).

In fact, Jesus' knowledge of Judas' involvement in the plot against Him explains the mysterious directions Jesus gave Peter and John regarding the preparation of the passover meal (Lk 22:7-13). Clearly, Jesus' purpose was to conceal the location from Judas.

Judas sold out his integrity for thirty pieces of silver. He betrayed himself and when he did, there remained within him, no self-respect, no honor, no truth of character. His capabilities became evident to him and when they did, it was more than he could bear. He returned to the chief priests, threw the silver down in the temple and left to hang himself (Matt 27:3-5). For Judas, returning the money and committing suicide was the only way of recovering balance within himself.

Admittedly, the example of Judas contains many extremes, but the point is clear. When God's people say one thing and do another, when they give the appearance of being one thing while practicing something completely different, there is an unsafe and potentially perilous imbalance. And while many people are affected by the hypocrisy, no one is affected more than the one creating the duplicity.

Those people who support an imbalance between their projected self and their real self will always bring some kind of discomfort and suffering upon themselves. But, God may also intervene when such a betrayal of self occurs.

The Hypocrisy of Ananias

When Ananias laid the proceeds from the sale of his property before the apostles' feet, the impression he gave concerning the gift was different from the gift itself. Peter responded,

> Ananias, why has Satan filled your heart to lie to the Holy Spirit and to keep back part of the proceeds of the land? While it remained unsold, did it not remain your own? And after it

was sold, was it not at your disposal? How is it that you have contrived this deed in your heart? You have not lied to men but to God (Acts 5:3-4).

In other words, Ananias could have done whatever he desired with the proceeds from the sale of the land. He could have kept none of it, a portion of it, or all of it. It did not matter. What was more important than Ananias' decision concerning the proceeds was the preservation of his character and his integrity. As it turns out, Ananias lied to himself, to the apostles and to God. The lie resulted in his death.

Ananias' hypocrisy serves to remind us of the tremendous amount of significance God places upon honesty, truthfulness and forthrightness. These are foundational for sound, healthy relationships, whether they be between friends, family members, or spouses. There is nothing that brings more hurt, more suspicion and more anguish than hypocrisy. There is nothing that more quickly drives a wedge, nothing that more quickly severs ties, nothing that more quickly creates an indefensible, even unresolvable position.

Often, as seen in the case of Ananias, the duplicity is unnecessary. Hurt is often inflicted upon a relationship for no good reason. The concealed thoughts and the hidden truths would do much less damage if they were simply brought into the open.

Admittedly, many people must learn how to be open. Through the years, they have either been silenced or ridiculed for their opinions, and as a result, they find it "safer" to remain quiet. However, these people can and must learn ways to express their feelings honestly while being sensitive to the emotions, opinions and needs of others.

Christians would do well to remember the words of Jesus which followed His warning to the disciples concerning hypocrisy when He said,

Nothing is covered up that will not be revealed, or hidden that will not be known. Whatever you have said in the dark shall be heard in the light, and what you have whispered in private rooms shall be proclaimed upon the housetops (Lk 12:2-3).

Basically, a person will respond to these words in one of two ways: either with great fear and trepidation or with a tremendous sense of relief. And depending upon the response, a person can learn much about himself.

On the one hand, if a person is fearful and anxious concerning these words of Jesus, obvious problems exist. Feelings of dread point to a person who has been less than honest with his intentions, less than kind with his words, and less than truthful about his agendas. Apprehension indicates a person who fears his hypocritical ways regarding relationships may one day be revealed.

On the other hand, a person may be relieved to hear these words, and this is good. This type of response points to a person who has kept his conscience clear, who believes that, one day, he will be exonerated regarding the false charges, insinuations and accusations leveled against him.

The person who responds to these words of Jesus with a sense of relief is one who hears, not words of indictment, but words which speak deliverance. This is the person who has allowed himself to be wronged, who has taken the blame when it rightly belonged elsewhere, who held his tongue to protect another even though his silence raised suspicions concerning himself.

For this person, Jesus' words point to justice, vindication, and acquittal. He hears words which point to the revelation of truth and concerning that revelation, there is not fear, but jubilation. There is not a sense of dis-ease, but of comfort. This is the person who conducts himself, to the best of his ability, in a manner that is appropriate before both God and humanity. The effort is sometimes great, but the rewards are always greater, in both this realm and the one to follow.

Jesus refers to hypocrisy as leaven, and this is appropriate, for hypocrisy is that which penetrates slowly but consistently. Hypocrisy is that which is capable of eroding first the soul, and eventually the entire church. Few things are more destructive to a person, and few things are more destructive to the community of believers than when God's people are saying one thing and practicing something else.

The Call For Sincerity

If there is any one thing that separates those who have encountered Jesus Christ from those who have not, that one thing must certainly be love. And love, while it remains the easiest thing to receive, is by far the most difficult to practice with any degree of proficiency. The truth of this statement becomes abundantly evident as we allow the commonly superficial perception of love to languish in the face of the scriptural command, "Let love be genuine" (Rom 12:9).

All too often, Christians feel they have scaled the heights of beneficence as they graciously maintain a congenial demeanor around those people with whom they have difficulty. The problem with this is that the congeniality is nothing more than a cleverly practiced facade. This being the case, the behavior is hardly laudable. On the contrary, such actions are to be lamented in that hypocrisy is indicated. And hypocrisy, as we have seen, is the antithesis of love.

There is not one person who would not see this as being very hard teaching. But, as it is clearly and repeatedly voiced by various portions of Scripture, the teaching most certainly remains. Therefore, those who search for acceptance would be well advised to take these lessons seriously.

Let love be genuine; hate what is evil, hold fast to what is good; love one another with brotherly affection; outdo one another in showing honor. Never flag in zeal, be aglow with the Spirit, serve the Lord. Rejoice in your hope, be patient in tribulation, be constant in prayer. Contribute to the needs of the saints, practice hospitality. Bless those who persecute you; bless and do not curse them. Rejoice with those who rejoice, weep with those who weep. Live in harmony with one another; do not be haughty, but associate with the lowly; never be conceited. Repay no one evil for evil, but take thought for what is noble in the sight of all. If possible, so far as it depends upon you, live peaceably with all. Beloved, never avenge yourselves, but leave it to the wrath of God; for it is written, "Vengeance is mine, I will repay, says the Lord." No, "if your enemy is hungry, feed him; if he is thirsty, give him drink; for by so doing you will heap burning coals upon his head. Do not be overcome by evil, but overcome evil with good (Rom 12:9-21).

Paul's words to the Roman church concerning love begin with a mandate regarding love's sincerity. If love is feigned in any direction or in any measure, it does not meet the scriptural definition of love. In fact, it is not love at all. It is pretense.

In Romans 12, Paul gives a short but profound definition of love. Then, just as quickly, he reminds his readers of what is to be their general attitude towards evil. After doing these two things, Paul speaks less generally, relating to the Romans how they are to conduct themselves as Christians. And he does so two ways: (1) by making reference to their expected behavior within the community of faith (Rom 12:9-13), and (2) by giving instruction concerning their participation in the lives of those who live outside the faith community (Rom 12:14-20).

Not surprisingly, Christians are to see themselves as a single entity, caring for one another more so than they care for themselves, contributing to one another's needs and being hospitable in every sense of the word. These words are received with little surprise. For most of us, the church is where our efforts are focused when it comes to practicing hospitality, patience, forgiveness, etc. But as we read further in Paul's letter, we realize, to our dismay, that our shortcomings within the church are only the beginning.

According to Paul, our efforts regarding the practice of love must extend into the lives of those who do not share our commitment to the person of Jesus Christ. In fact, Paul goes further to say we must love those who oppose our way of life, even persecute us for our beliefs. The words found in Romans 12 could not be any clearer. Look at the following five commands expressed by Paul over just seven verses:

1) Bless those who persecute you; bless and do not curse them (verse 14).

2) Repay no one evil for evil, but take thought for what is noble in the sight of all (verse 17).

3) If possible, so far as it depends upon you, live peaceably with all (verse 18).

4) Beloved, never avenge yourselves, but leave it to the wrath of God; for it is written, "Vengeance is mine, I will repay, says the Lord" (verse 19).

5) No, "if your enemy is hungry, feed him; if he is thirsty, give him drink; for by so doing you will heap burning coals upon his head" (verse 20).

Clearly, these are not random ramblings, but literary insertions deliberately stacked for the purpose of leaving no doubt as to how Christians are to treat and respond to those who practice evil. On the one hand, Christians must never embrace or tolerate evil. But on the other hand, they must love those involved in the activity.

Reading these verses should be a sobering exercise, but even more when we remember how Paul introduced his thoughts when he said, "let love be genuine." In other words, our conduct inside and outside the church must not only be exemplary, but that which has love as its base. And love never has anything to do with pretense and hypocrisy. If a Christian is practicing these before ANY person, that Christian does not have the kind of love of which is spoken in the Scriptures.

Without question, the incorporation of love is one of the most difficult things for Christians. If it only involved a change of behavior, it would be relatively simple. But, a person's conduct is not where the essence of love is found, only its manifestation.

Love demands a transformation of the spirit. And when this transformation takes place, there is no longer any need for deception and pretense. When a person is truly practicing a love that is genuine, there no longer remains any reason to fabricate and mislead, delude and beguile. Everything is in the open, and with this predominating location of the self, there is liberation that can only be understood by those who have experienced it.

Love does not cry for vengeance; there is no need. Love does not seek retribution, nor does it require justice. Love has a single task, and that is to uplift; it has a single goal, and that is to inspire; it has a single intention, and that is to sustain. If there is one thing that separates those who are born of Jesus Christ from those who are not, it most certainly is love. It is indeed the only thing capable of overcoming the evil that is all too pervasive.

Manifesting The New Life

People are interesting. When there is opportunity to either denigrate or uplift, they choose the former; when there exists the option to either ignore or become actively involved, again, they choose the former. When they have the ability to shield, they opt instead to make vulnerable. And when they have opportunity to speak favorably, they choose instead to keep silent. This is not the love of which the Bible speaks.

1 Corinthians 13 is, arguably, the most important of all chapters in the Bible. It provides what is essential instruction for those who expect to become what God would have them be. The tremendous significance attached to love is expressed by Paul in the first several verses.

> If I speak in the tongues of men and of angels, but have not love, I am a noisy gong or a clanging cymbal. And if I have prophetic powers, and understand all mysteries and all knowledge, and if I have all faith, so as to remove mountains, but have not love, I am nothing. If I give away all I have, and if I deliver my body to be burned, but have not love, I gain nothing (1 Cor 13:1-3).

Whereas some faith communities practice the various spiritual gifts as though they alone are capable of closing the chasm that exists between heaven and earth, according to the apostle Paul, the importance of spiritual gifts pale in comparison to love. Without love, a person's very existence is without meaning. Paul explains this to the Corinthians, then tells them what love is.

"Love is patient and kind"

When a person thinks of being patient, many different scenarios and circumstances come to mind. Perhaps the most difficult has to do with waiting on the Lord for that which we are convinced is God's will.

For example, Jeremiah waited upon God decade after decade, waiting to see the people of Judah come to a place where they were serving God. Most people would agree it must have been God's will for Jeremiah to accomplish the purpose of his calling, that being the salvation of the people. But, as it turned out, Jeremiah never could get the people to listen.

Being patient, when it is much easier to become frustrated or disheartened, is one of the more difficult tasks for any Christian. This kind of patience is possible only for those who possess a certain kind of trust--the trust which persists even though prevailing circumstances point to an opposite response. Jeremiah was a person with such trust.

Jeremiah prophesied to the people of Judah for years and years concerning the judgment that would befall them if they did not alter their attitudes and their deeds. When the judgment of God finally fell and the city of Jerusalem was devastated by the Babylonians, Jeremiah surveyed the desolation and wrote in response to what he saw.

The roads to Zion mourn, for none come to the appointed feasts; all her gates are desolate, her priests groan; her maidens have been dragged away, and she herself suffers bitterly. Her foes have become the head, her enemies prosper, because the LORD has made her suffer for the multitude of her transgressions; her children have gone away, captives before the foe. From the daughter of Zion has departed all her majesty. Her princes have become like harts that find no pasture; they fled without strength before the pursuer. Jerusalem remembers in the days of her affliction and bitterness all the precious things that were hers from days of old. When her people fell into the hand of the foe, and there was none to help her, the foe gloated over her, mocking at her downfall. Jerusalem sinned grievously, therefore she became filthy; all who honored her despise her, for they have seen her nakedness; yea, she herself groans, and turns her face away. Her uncleanness was in her skirts; she took no thought of her doom; therefore her fall is terrible, she has no comforter" (Lam 1:4-9).

There was no person who better understood the failure of the people of Judah. Jeremiah himself had failed miserably in his task to turn these people around. And what a depressing sight this must have been for Jeremiah, staring out over the once great city, having, among other things, the failure of his efforts looming before him with such great clarity. But, incredibly, in the face of so much dis-ease, the prophet is able to look upward and say,

The steadfast love of the LORD never ceases, his mercies never come to an end; they are new every morning; great is thy faithfulness. "The LORD is my portion," says my soul, "therefore I will hope in him" (Lam 3:22-24).

Jeremiah had every earthly reason to cry out in protest against a God who called him to give up so much for so many years, only to have the result of his efforts laying painfully before him in a pile of blood-stained rubble once called Jerusalem. But, there were no cries of injustice, no words of criticism--only a confident response of trust born, not of what was seen, but of what was unseen.

So often, people will not understand that discomfort and even tragedy are often necessary components in a larger plan designed to usher in moments of tremendous triumph and miraculous transformations. Unfortunately, people see with their eyes and feel with their emotions all the while missing the undercurrent of God's presence and purpose. "Patience" assists a person in his ability to capture the reality of that undercurrent.

If love is patient, then a person in possession of love must trust God to bring about that which is meaningful and purpose-filled, regardless of the seeming absence and impotence of His power and work. But, if love is patient, it is also that which allows a person to treat his enemies as Paul prescribes in his letter to the Romans, with respect and humility and kindness. It is that which allows a person the ability to endure insult, rejection and neglect, knowing that one day, justice will come to the fore, and all wrongdoing will be made right.

There is no person who does not see the various injustices of life. And there is no person who does not personally experience such injustices along with the accompanying bewilderment and the distress. That the injustices will come is not in question; what is in question is how people respond.

For some, the distress is debilitating, wearing upon them until faith and hope and trust are all but non-existent. But for others, the spirit is able to carry the person above the impending crisis, defeating that which would weaken, frustrate and eventually subdue others.

Accompanying the kind of love of which Paul speaks in 1 Corinthians 13, there is patience. It is a patience that stands firmly against seeming failures, patience that stands firmly in the face of great injustices and patience that remains kind to those who produce and perpetuate distressful and uncomfortable moments.

The patience of which Paul speaks in his correspondence to the Corinthians is to be practiced even with those who are ungodly and seemingly incorrigible. Very simply, concerning these people, we are to "believe all things and hope all things" (1 Cor 13:7).

Most people are familiar with the pain that accompanies emotional injuries inflicted upon them repeatedly by someone close to them. And most, again, are familiar with the feelings of betrayal that produce an unwillingness to direct any kind of emotional energy toward that person; it becomes much easier and safer to simply shut off completely. It is concluded that, without expectations, there exists no possibility of disappointment. Although this reaction is understandable, and not by any means infrequent, it runs contrary to the direction given by the apostle Paul in his letter to the Corinthians.

The person who is unwilling to place himself in any kind of emotional risk is a person who runs another danger, that being the negation of the God-given faculty for the enjoyment of life itself. A person can perhaps protect himself to a certain degree from the hurt and the pain, but what inevitably accompanies such a procedure is a dampening of the emotions that make a person feel alive.

"Shutting down" and being emotionally "hidden" is not in keeping with either God's Word or God's character. God's people are to "believe all things and hope all things." In other words, they are to hold out hope, not just in a cerebral sense, but in an emotional sense; not just in a general sense, but in a personal sense.

Forgiving our brother "seventy times seven" times has much less to do with mouthing words than it does the state of the soul--that state of apprehension concerning the fact that our brother will change, that he will one day undergo a transformation. For God's people to hold out hope in this regard, there is required a patient hope that, again, transcends anything we can receive from our earthly existence; it is indeed a divine exercise--and one in which we are able to participate.

"Love is not jealous or boastful, arrogant or rude"

Jesus Christ and the Bible both have an illuminating quality that all people, if they are honest, find to be at the very least unsettling, perhaps downright disturbing. This is good because it means the divine revelatory encounter these people are experiencing is having its desired effect.

Jesus Christ and the Bible possess a unique ability to create an extremely important reference point. As previously discussed, people's realities are so compelling, they are unable to perceive outside their own perimeter of experience. This is not good in that settled perceptions need challenging or there is contentment where there could be growth; there is passivity where there should be action.

For example, some people, even Christian people, cannot begin to fathom an existence where people are more concerned about others than themselves. People's self-contained, self-referential, self-serving lives are so inescapably looped back to themselves, that the state and condition of others is not only of secondary importance, but at times, altogether unimportant. As we have already seen in Paul's letter to the Romans,

> Bless those who persecute you; bless and do not curse them. Rejoice with those who rejoice, weep with those who weep. Live in harmony with one another; do not be haughty, but associate with the lowly; never be conceited. Repay no one evil for evil, but take thought for what is noble in the sight of all. If possible, so far as it depends upon you, live peaceably with all (Rom 12:14-18).

This portion of Scripture leaves the unmistakable impression that living in "harmony" and "peace" with one another goes far beyond the avoidance of public conflict and quarrel. "Rejoicing with those who rejoice" and "weeping with those who weep" indicates a relationship that goes far beyond cordiality and tolerance; it indicates a concerned empathy that displaces passionate pride, a loving consideration that stands in the place of self-serving egotism.

Taking thought "for what is noble" in other people is a mental exercise wholly peculiar to many people. What is much more familiar is the tendency to discover and subsequently elevate all that is ignoble in other people. What is much more normative is to discern that which is undesirable and speak it into the realm of contemptibility, to ascertain a weakness and advance it to a place of complete loathsomeness.

Clearly, the love of which the apostle Paul speaks is one that lays aside jealousy and boastfulness, arrogance and rudeness. There is no room for these in that the interests and well-being of others take a predominating, even all-encompassing position. The possession of such a "default" is foreign to most, a pipedream to many, something strived for by only a few.

Jesus Christ in particular and the Bible in general bring this perspective to life for us. They provide evidence, not only of the possibility of such selflessness, but of the unmistakable reality of its existence. Most are put to shame as they compare their petty, selfish thoughts and concerns to the amazing benevolence and compassion of the many biblical characters, not the least of whom is Jesus Christ. Such demonstrations can only be born in the heart of God.

"Love does not insist on its own way"

A person makes a promising step towards breaking from his self-serving lifestyle when he accepts Jesus Christ into his life. This acceptance is no small matter in that more is involved than a mental assent concerning the divinity and/or salvific quality of Jesus Christ. Beyond this, there is a commitment of the heart, an acquiescence of the spirit and a resignation of the will. Whereas simple belief is of fundamental importance, more is required. And this is where most would-be Christians falter. It is not easy to allow someone else to control that which, for so long, has been theirs to direct and inform.

It is one thing for a person to subordinate his will to God. This is difficult enough. But it is an entirely different matter for a person to subordinate his will to others, for this, in a very real sense, is a subordination of the self, an exercise tantamount to subservience. But this is precisely what love is.

As Jesus Christ was willing to empty Himself of the self-governing exercise of His divine power (Phil 2:7), becoming a servant in the form of a man, so must we be willing to empty ourselves of the self-governing quality to which we have grown so accustomed.

When Jesus was in the garden of Gethsemane (Matt 26:36ff), He was clearly disturbed by the reality of the cross. It was probably not so much the thought of physical pain or death as it was the prospect of being without the Father immediately prior to and during His death. Jesus clearly understood that the person of God and the reality of sin were wholly incompatible and therefore, could not possibly inhabit the same space. If Jesus were to accept the sins of the world, the Father would have no choice but to reject Jesus.

But, as unsettling as this was to Jesus, as much as He did not want to go through with it, He bowed His will to the will of the Father. In the garden, Jesus prayed, "My Father, if it be possible, let this cup pass from me; nevertheless, not as I will, but as thou wilt" (Matt 26:39).

Christians and non-Christians alike are ignorant as to the benefits of God's presence in their lives. Christians are daily unaware of the unsearchable activity of God's Spirit on their behalf. And non-Christians also profit greatly from the divine presence in this world. Without it, unholy powers would wield their misfortune at will, wreaking havoc that can only be imagined. Indeed, God's grace is a living, dynamic force in the world, providing an effective buffer between humanity and the powers that would destroy.

The apostle Paul tells us that "love does not insist on its own way." If we are in possession of such love, it means, simply, that we become as Jesus was. Jesus subordinated His will to the will of the Father as He placed Himself in a position of ultimate subservience. In the same act of humiliation, Jesus demonstrated perfect obedience to God and a prototypical servility to humanity.

The love of which the apostle Paul speaks calls for us to place ourselves last. Both the desires of God and the needs of others must take priority over our own wants and requirements. And this means that we do not only seek to place others first, but that we actively pursue avenues which bring others gratification and fulfillment. "Love does not insist on its own way."

"Love is not irritable or resentful"

Albeit a generalization, it is for the most part true: people are far too sensitive. The uncertainties and hesitancies people have concerning themselves make it nearly impossible, at times, for others to do anything but respond with the same tentativeness and doubt. Every word must be questioned before it is uttered; possible reactions and interpretations need to be examined and various consequences weighed. Because of such sensitivity, relationships become strained, at times irreconcilable.

A person who is not "irritable" is one whose level of sensitivity is not the consistent cause of conflict and quarrel. This is a person who does not provoke the sensitivity of others, and by others does not have his own defense mechanisms and passions easily aroused. Simply put, hard feelings are not routinely the result of his participation in group activity.

Everyone has experienced the discomfort that goes with "walking on eggshells" around a person who is constantly getting upset and frustrated and angry. This is the person who is sure he is being slighted or left out; somehow, he is being disregarded or snubbed. It is nothing if not uncomfortable and the result is a dampening effect on whatever activity is in place.

Obviously, a person such as this one has many problems to sort out. Clearly, he is far too irritable and easily provoked. And while interacting with such a person presents some challenges, it also provides excellent opportunity for others to gauge their own level of "irritability." In fact, no better occasion exists for a person to measure his own level of sensitivity. And this is how relating to such a person should be viewed, not as an inconvenience to be shunned, but a challenge to be overcome.

According to Paul, love is not "irritable." It is also not "resentful," which is to say that love does not take into account a wrong suffered. And the most poignant expression of this is found in none other than Jesus Christ.

It is truly amazing what was suffered by Jesus. From the beginning of His ministry to the end, he was mocked and scorned by nearly everyone with whom He came in contact. From those in His home town who "took offense at Him" (Mark 6:3) to His family members who said He was "beside himself" (Mark 3:21) which is to say He was insane, to those before whom He stood with a crown of thorns and a cloak of mockery who cried, "Crucify Him! Crucify Him!" to the despicable thief on the cross next to Him who taunted Him with the words, "Are you not the Christ? Save yourself and us!" (Lk 23:39) What was Jesus' response to all of this abuse? "Father, forgive them for they know not what they do" (Lk 23:34).

Jesus Christ truly epitomizes a spirit that does not take into account a wrong suffered. Unquestionably, there is sharp contrast between such beneficence and the accounting taken by most people who have wrongs suffered against them.

What is often true is that people, at any and every opportunity, use the past mistakes of others as weapons against them; people do not know how to allow past offenses to be forgotten. Instead, these offenses are brought to the surface whenever some kind of leverage is required. Such behavior runs directly counter to the divine will and character. In fact, there are few things that more clearly represent what God is not.

Being in possession of the love of which Paul speaks means that we are not people who provoke others, taking advantage of their weaknesses and errors. Furthermore, we are not easily provoked by others, but instead, remain calm in the face of transparent attempts to disturb our God-given serenity. And finally, although people, even those self-proclaimed "righteous" ones, refuse to give us opportunity to move beyond past mistakes and errors, we must forget the hurts and the pain inflicted upon us, regardless of whether or not those inflictions were intentional. We must stand resolute in our determination to harbor no grudge, to take into account no wrong, to forget whatever transgression may have been committed against us. It is only then that we are able to stand before God with any measure of self-respect.

"Love does not rejoice at wrong, but rejoices in the right"

This is an area in every person's life that requires close examination. And what must be understood before anything else is that Paul is not saying, "We must not applaud sin and transgression but only those things which are pleasing to God." This would be stating the obvious.

The comment Paul is making has more to do with the way we respond and give voice to those things which are undesirable, unsightly and ungodly. Unfortunately, people are not fully aware of how their expressions are capable of validating certain events and happenings.

For example, in the case of an unsightly rumor, even if the story is prefaced with a disclaimer along the lines of "I am not sure if this is true or not," the expression of the rumor's content brings a certain validity to it that was not there previously.

And the sad truth is, people enjoy the misfortunes and the mishaps of others. They enjoy speaking of another person's calamity, either because their possession of information makes them feel a little more powerful or because they feel their own character is somehow elevated in the face of another person's misfortune.

For whatever reason, many people are attuned to the undesirable and the catastrophic. Mention a person's name and instead of hearing accolades concerning that person, negative comments about that person are heard. These are the people who see everything through a very strange, pessimistic, even cynical lens. And these people are, for the most part, completely oblivious to their ungodly perceptions, always seeing the negative, always forecasting the cataclysmic, always remembering the catastrophic.

This particular perspective exists primarily because of a spiritual problem. It is not due to a lack of positive, godly stimuli in this world, for the miraculous wonder of God is everywhere at any given time. But for whatever reason, there are those who do not easily assimilate the awesome workings of God.

Those who possess "love" are not so quick to judge, revile and condemn. They do not easily lose hope in God and humanity. They "believe all things," knowing that "in everything God works for good with those who love him, who are called according to his purpose" (Rom 8:28). And for these reasons, it is a relatively simple matter to remain confident, perceiving God, world and self in an optimistic, affirming and enthusiastic manner.

For those who are unable to perceive and translate life in this way, there is a disturbing lack of God's presence. Clearly, God's Spirit is not allowed to sufficiently intermingle with their own. There is a distinct absence of the hope and the belief and the patience which all accompany God's love.

"Love bears all things, believes all things, hopes all things, endures all things."

These words, as are the others we have examined, are written in the context of relationships being established and sustained. At no time can Paul's words be decoded into a situation where there is any measure of isolation. In a context such as this, no sense can be made of the direction Paul offers.

For whatever reason, people often operate with two basic inclinations at the ready. First, they observe and subsequently publicize the weaknesses and transgressions of others. And secondly, they are guarded, at times overly defensive concerning the same scrutiny being directed toward themselves. It is completely ironic that such close scrutiny and subsequent publicization is perceived as harmless when it is practiced by a person and directed elsewhere. But when that same person becomes the object of such behavior, the activity is perceived to be not only annoying, but invasive, even threatening.

Those who number among the woefully disadvantaged in this world are those who understand how they are hurt by others but do not take this information and use it to modify the way they treat others. Hurt is understood to be applicable only to themselves. They have great difficulty escaping the psychological snare that causes people to treat others only as they themselves are treated. This is a vicious circle that is only broken by deliberate, pro-active effort. Anything less simply feeds, and subsequently strengthens the circle.

To "bear all things, believe all things, hope all things and endure all things," is to escape from the ironic entanglement in which so many people find themselves. To practice these means that the insecure relationship with self is set aside as efforts are instead focused toward the support, maintenance and promotion of the well being and self-esteem of others.

To "bear" all things means to overlook error rather than highlight it, to give the benefit of the doubt rather than drive the nail of condemnation. All too often, people are offered no hope and given no second chances. Instead, those who are guilty or presumed guilty are relegated to that position permanently. And unfortunately, this is done with all too much ease.

Concerning transgression, people generally find it easier to accuse rather than overlook, to condemn rather than forgive. With most people, even "Christian" people, it is easier to point the finger rather than make polite inquiries, easier to hold a grudge rather than forgive. This is completely contradictory in that Christians should be involved in granting absolution to those who sinned against them.

There are many different ways to sin but basically, people either sin against God or against one another. This being the case, then forgiveness must come from either God or people. Both, therefore, have the power to erase transgression. And while God is quick to forgive, perhaps quicker than He should be at times, people, on the other hand, are slow to offer pardon.

What many do not realize is that it is possible to be too concerned with "justice", too consumed by what is legally, even morally correct. What is often true is that a situation calls for nothing more than plain and simple forgiveness. Even when one party is clearly and admittedly "wrong," the other, at times, has a simple responsibility. That responsibility is to forgive.

Forgiveness must be offered with no ulterior motives, no expectations of return, no anticipation of anything other than resolution. Absolving others of sin clears that person's conscience and allows that person to stand before God without the weight of that particular transgression. Additionally, the person who forgives is, in a very real sense, finding forgiveness himself. Jesus said,

> For if you forgive men their trespasses, your heavenly Father also will forgive you; but if you do not forgive men their trespasses, neither will your Father forgive your trespasses (Matt 6:14).

Every person shares a responsibility toward one another to absolve of sin. As far as it is humanly possible, people must release others from the bondage that comes with wrongdoing, whether that wrongdoing is deliberate or unintentional. God has done far more than what could possibly be expected of Him to discard the guilt of those who have sinned against Him. People must be willing to do the same.

To "believe" all things is to hold out fundamental hope for all humankind. Within the nucleus of true Christianity, there is no room for cynicism, pessimism or even doubt. A person in possession of God's love is one who recognizes that with God, nothing is impossible. This means that there is no such thing as a "lost cause," or a "hopeless case." Suspicious, pessimistic and scornful spirits do not exist in the eternity of God. In fact, there is nothing that more thoroughly disrupts the love that is designed to flow from God to His own people and beyond.

To "hope" all things is to know that failure is never final. For example, it would be a simple matter to look to Jeremiah's life and see decades of failure and nothing more. And while it may be that little if no part of Jeremiah's ministry found much root, the person who "hopes" is one who maintains without doubting, that Jeremiah's so-called "failures" are already filled with consequences of tremendous value. Therefore, it is concluded that outgrowths and ramifications of Jeremiah's efforts are decidedly successful, regardless of outward appearance.

God is always successful and those who participate in God's plan will be triumphant as well. Conquest may be replete with failure, but in the end, there is yet conquest. The person who "hopes" is one who knows that God's triumph is sure, and therefore, what is seen and heard and felt is of secondary importance to the "hope" that remains.

To "endure" all things is to bring back our discussion regarding endurance and perseverance. Love is to "endure" in many ways. It is that which remains in the face of rejection and ridicule. It is that which combats the feeling of being overwhelmed or dismayed. There is an "endurance" that forgives again and again, trusting that the next time, there will be no need to offer it. With love, there is a persistence concerning our own shortcomings and the imperfections of others. "Love" never ceases to try in countless directions.

Love speaks primarily to the relationships developed between people. Naturally, it also relates to our association with God and to the relationship we have with ourselves, but for the most part, our lives line up with Paul's delineation of love as our relationships with one another are affected. We must remember that the words of 1 Corinthians 13 are not the ramblings of an idealist, but the sincere renderings of a man who knew the freedom associated with a relationship and comprehension of the divine mind.

Paul tells us that "love never ends" (1 Cor 13:8). Although there are many finite things around which love revolves, it is only love which has an enduring quality. Naturally, people should exert more effort concerning the development and maintenance of those things infinite, not temporary. If this be the case, the love of which the apostle Paul speaks MUST be a priority, for it has an unending quality that stretches into the eternity of God.

Community Interaction

As mentioned in the previous section, love is, for all practical purposes, meaningless in the context of isolation. Directives and direction concerning love have no sensible platform if there is no one to receive its benefits and its message.

While it is certainly true that love is something that exists all by itself, requiring no object for its essence and its continuance, it is also true that love's appropriate arena is the community. If love is to be effective and fruitful, as God intends it to be, it then requires an object, that which gives love an opportunity to touch and to influence, to encourage and to challenge, to arouse and inspire. Only within the community does such opportunity exist.

Lessons from 1 Kings

In chapter 17 of 1 Kings, there are three interlocking stories which, on the surface, relate the power of God and the miracles produced by His prophet Elijah. Beneath the surface, we discover that many issues are being explored which encompass the musings of all generations. Examined are matters related to life and death, the various manifestations of divine sovereignty and the tremendous significance concerning the interrelationships of God's people.

An exploration regarding God Himself probably lies even deeper within these narratives. As we pursue this avenue, we see how God is able to bring forth whatever He desires: hardship, joy, distress and well-being. But in the end, we learn what we probably knew all along, that God is consistently determined to produce that which is related to life.

Chapter 17 begins with Elijah announcing that a drought will cover the land. After disclosing this information, God directs the prophet to a location where he might escape the effects of the drought.

> And the word of the LORD came to him, "Depart from here and turn eastward, and hide yourself by the brook Cherith, that is east of the Jordan. You shall drink from the brook, and I have commanded the ravens to feed you there" (1 Kgs 17:2-4).

And all went according to God's word. Elijah isolated himself by the brook and for a time, the water and the ravens supplied him with everything he needed to survive. After a time, the brook dried and Elijah was instructed to journey to a city where a widow had been prepared to nourish him.

> So he arose and went to Zarephath; and behold, a widow was there gathering sticks; and he called to her and said, "Bring me a little water in a vessel, that I may drink." And as she was going to bring it, he called to her and said, "Bring me a morsel of bread in your hand." And she said, "As the LORD your God lives, I have nothing baked, only a handful of meal in a jar, and little oil in a cruse; and now, I am gathering a couple of sticks, that I may go in and prepare it for myself and my son, that we may eat it, and die" (1 Kgs 17:10-12).

The reader has no choice but to count this chain of events as being something other than coincidental. For an unspecified amount of time, Elijah was sitting by the brook and when there was absolutely no more water, he was instructed to go to a place where a widow and her son were down to what was absolutely their final meal. In the widow's mind, her and her son's fate was so final that she recounted to Elijah her very simple, very fatalistic plan: to eat one last meal and die.

By means of the brook and the ravens, God provided for Elijah for a time. For whatever reason, God decided it was time for Elijah and the widow to provide for one another. If Elijah was unwilling to assist the widow, he would die. The same held true if the widow was unwilling to help Elijah.

> And Elijah said to her, "Fear not; go and do as you have said; but first make me a little cake of it and bring it to me, and afterward make for yourself and your son. For thus says the LORD the God of Israel, `The jar of meal shall not be spent, and the cruse of oil shall not fail, until the day that the LORD sends rain upon the earth.'" And she went and did as Elijah said; and she, and he, and her household ate for many days. The jar of meal was not spent, neither did the cruse of oil fail, according to the word of the LORD which he spoke by Elijah (1 Kgs 17:13-16).

Obviously, God played an important role in the survival of the three people but without their willingness to provide assistance to one another, God's role would have been insufficient. Details concerning the woman's life are absent, but what is very clear is that she had no difficulty providing water for herself, her son and the prophet. Elijah had no water, but was able to bring food to the table. Together, the widow and Elijah survive.

What is learned from this story can be a bit puzzling to some, but probably because they presuppose God to be a celestial bread merchant, somehow appointed to relieve all hunger in the world. From the first two stories in 1 Kings 17, we find God to be slightly more complex.

There is no denying that God was responsible for the drought in the first place. It was by His word that the drought came into being, but it was also by His word that the drought would end. What is also true is that God provided for His people during time of drought. He supernaturally intervened, not only for those supposedly "closer" to Him, like the prophet Elijah, but the poor widow as well. Clearly, there was a divine willingness to sustain people, but only to a certain extent. At times, God expects His people to uphold and preserve themselves, and this by mutual effort.

This story serves as a reminder that God intervenes on behalf of His people, but it also demonstrates there are times when God does not. The reasons for this are easier to accept when adversity is absent, but the reasons yet remain. If not for the struggles in a person's life, there would be no growth, no character development and no increase in a person's faith. Only when people are confronted by opposition do they have opportunity to be strengthened. Without struggle, there cannot possibly be maturation and growth.

> Count it all joy, my brethren, when you meet various trials, for you know that the testing of your faith produces steadfastness. And let steadfastness have its full effect, that you may be perfect and complete, lacking in nothing (James 1:2-4).

> [Y]ou, who by God's power are guarded through faith for a salvation ready to be revealed in the last time. In this you rejoice, though now for a little while you may have to suffer various trials, so that the genuineness of your faith, more precious than gold which though perishable is tested by fire, may redound to praise and glory and honor at the revelation of Jesus Christ (1 Pet 1:5-7).

As God's people go through life, there is an inevitable and necessary struggle. God is there to assist His people in their adversities but a divinely conceived interdependency among God's people is also in place. God's sovereignty insists His people are to be mutually reliant and supportive of one another. And to ignore this interdependency is to deprive oneself of God-ordained provision.

The first two stories of 1 Kings 17 make it clear that God often times allows His people to struggle. But what is also clear is that God chooses life for His people, not death, as seen in the examples of Elijah and the widow. God's ways are various when it comes to sustaining His people, but what remains is that God sustains them. This is brought into even sharper focus in the third story found in chapter 17.

> After this the son of the woman, the mistress of the house, became ill; and his illness was so severe that there was no breath left in him. And she said to Elijah, "What have you against me, O man of God? You have come to me to bring my sin to remembrance, and to cause the death of my son!" (1 Kgs 17:17-18)

Most are familiar with how Elijah took the widow's son, carried him to the upper chamber and laid him on the bed. Elijah stretched himself out upon him three times and cried, "O LORD my God, let this child's soul come into him again" (1 Kgs 17:22). The prophet's prayer was answered and the widow's son was returned to her.

Clearly, the way Elijah stretched himself out upon the widow's son was to demonstrate the prophet's intimate involvement and concern regarding the situation. There is no question that God intervened, but there is also no question that Elijah was there, assisting, supporting and sustaining to the very best of his emotional and spiritual abilities.

To fully understand the teaching of these three interwoven stories, it is helpful to know that the widow's home, Zarephath, was located in the country of Sidon, which was not what one would consider God's country. The people here practiced a way of life that ran contrary to God's precepts. Everything about them was pagan, their religion, their culture, their entire way of life.

The widow of Sidon numbered among those who were opposed to Elijah's God, but when she and her son were down to their last meal, God appeared through the person of Elijah and brought deliverance and well-being. The widow was sustained and her son who was raised to worship Baal was restored after his death. God appeared and when He did, life appeared with Him.

All too often, the people of our day find it so much easier to be judgmental and unforgiving. Every one of us, at times, find it all too convenient to be critical and non-supportive. It is easier to walk away than it is to become involved.

It must be remembered that there is a God-given interdependence among us, and not just when we are in the company of those who possess beliefs and values similar to our own. The message God provides is that we are responsible for one another. And with this responsibility comes the need to be encouraging, sympathetic and understanding. Concerning others, there must be a focus, not upon the frailties, the weaknesses and the errors, but on the needs, the possibilities and the potential. Only then do we become people who reflect the true image of God, a God who remains forever committed to life.

Lessons from 1 Corinthians

One of the many handicaps faced by faith communities is a common misperception regarding diversity within the body of Christ. In many cases, diversity is viewed as that which is to be scaled, classified, arranged and otherwise categorized. And all this for the purpose of ranking the members according to some person's perception of relative worth.

From Paul's first letter to the Corinthians, we discover there is nothing more absurd than this conception of diversity, nothing more inimical to God's intended purpose for the body of believers, that purpose being the edification and maturation of the congregation along with the glorification of the lordship of Jesus Christ.

Diversity testifies, not only to the creativity of God, but also to His resourcefulness. When one considers that every one of God's creations is uniquely different from all the rest, this by itself is spectacular. But beyond this, God is able to take His people, with their various exceptional qualities, and meld them into a body of believers suitable for productive service in the world. God can successfully take a multitude of individuals and fashion them together in such a way as to make them an effective, even supreme force in both temporal and spiritual realms. And when the body of Christ becomes something other than effective and productive, it is never the result of divine failing, but human.

> Now there are varieties of gifts, but the same Spirit; and there are varieties of service, but the same Lord; and there are varieties of working, but it is the same God who inspires them all in every one. To each is given the manifestation of the Spirit for the common good (1 Cor 12:4-7).

The gifts and the ministries of God's people are never intended to be any kind of badge indicating honor or recognition or worth. On the contrary, their focus is always the effect or consequence of their performance. And for the successful operation of these gifts or services or workings, only God is worthy to receive recognition and thanksgiving.

Clearly, any of these manifestations among the members of the body of Christ begins and ends with God.   God alone is the inspirational force; God alone is responsible for giving their expression an opportunity.

In light of these truths, there is no room for the arrogance which accompanies so many of God's gifts and ministries.   For whatever reason, members who are used as conduits of God's accomplished purpose consider themselves more special than the other members.   In the same way, there is no room for envy in the body of Christ.   This emotion betrays the idea that certain positions and responsibilities are to be captured as trophies to be displayed and admired.

From prison, the apostle Paul addressed the Philippian church's concern regarding the variety of motivations that led men to preach the message of Jesus Christ.

> Some indeed preach Christ from envy and rivalry, but others from good will. The latter do it out of love, knowing that I am put here for the defense of the gospel; the former proclaim Christ out of partisanship, not sincerely but thinking to afflict me in my imprisonment. What then? Only that in every way, whether in pretense or in truth, Christ is proclaimed; and in that I rejoice (Phil 1:15-18).

From Paul's words, it can be surmised that the person carrying the message is clearly secondary in importance to the message itself. Paul only cared that "in every way, whether in pretense or in truth," Christ was proclaimed.

Those members of Christ's body who are used by God to manifest His will and purpose are best viewed as willing vessels, nothing more. And this willingness deserves little recognition, for it is the very least God's people can do in light of what they have received from Him.

Because we are brought up in a culture where excellence is measured by another person's defeat, we naturally compare and contrast ourselves with one another. This is fine as long as the process serves as a catalyst for self-improvement, but when feelings of deficiency and failure, even resentment result, there is something fundamentally wrong with the procedure.

God did not intend His people to measure themselves against one another and to subsequently make determinations concerning relative importance and degree of significance. According to the apostle Paul, determinations such as these are wholly inappropriate.

> But as it is, God arranged the organs in the body, each one of them, as he chose. If all were a single organ, where would the body be? As it is, there are many parts, yet one body. The eye cannot say to the hand, "I have no need of you," nor again the head to the feet, "I have no need of you." On the contrary, the parts of the body which seem to be weaker are indispensable, and those parts of the body which we think less honorable we invest with the greater honor, and our unpresentable parts are treated with greater modesty, which our more presentable parts do not require. But God has so adjusted the body, giving the greater honor to the inferior part, that there may be no discord in the body, but that the members may have the same care for one another. If one member suffers, all suffer together; if one member is honored, all rejoice together (1 Cor 12:18-26).

The divine plan concerning the body of Christ has within its rudimentary structure, a concern and attitude revolving around the group, not the individual. Whereas humanity is guilty of injecting concepts such as positioning, ranking and classifying, God restores balance by "giving the greater honor to the inferior part, that there may be no discord in the body" (verse 24).

If the concerns of the members of Christ are to parallel the concerns of God, then interests regarding position, honor and ranking must be dispelled. They must be displaced by a concern for the common good and the lordship of Jesus Christ. These concerns epitomize the purpose of the body of Christ in that the congregation receives spiritual sustenance and Christ receives exaltation.

Christians would do well to remember it is God who makes determinations and decisions concerning the body of Christ. A person is chosen to fill a gap, certainly because of ability but more because a particular gap exists. As long as there is a void, the body of Christ is inoperative in a certain direction. Because God determines the various directions the body of Christ must take, it only stands to reason God must also be responsible for filling the gaps. Clearly, He is the only one who has the necessary awareness to do so.

Given all this, human aspirations within the body of Christ are, in a very real sense, interference with the divine will. Anything even closely resembling ambitions or yearnings must therefore be inspired by God.

Because the body of Christ must reflect the mind of God and not the projections of any one individual or group of individuals, at no time must members take it upon themselves to make determinations concerning who is and is not allowed to participate. Any interference along these lines brings sure and certain disruption.

The sooner the church is able to disassociate itself from yearnings related to success, prosperity and competition, the sooner it can approach the model laid down for them by the apostle Paul in his first letter to the Corinthians. Members of the church must develop the same attitude God has regarding the body of Christ. The "common good" and the "lordship of Christ" must dominate their thinking and rule their actions. Selfish ambition, arrogance and envy will destroy what God has worked so diligently to build through His Son. Therefore, they must be cast off, and done so permanently.

Concluding Comments

Much has been examined in this chapter but perhaps the most succinct way of summarizing its reflections is to say that within the church of Jesus Christ, there must exist a genuine love that springs from a community spirit.

This is difficult when one considers the pervasive absence of sincerity, the ubiquitous glorification of the self and the all-encompassing decadence that so permeate this earthly sphere. Given these sad truths as our framework, it is a wonder we can survive as Christians at all. But survive we must.

As discussed previously, people become who God would have them when divine accomplishment is coupled with human effort. This effort can and must take many forms, but none can be quite as potentially meaningful as when a person seeks to exemplify the very person of Christ.

In the next chapter, we will be looking at the Christ-hymn found in Philippians 2. There is perhaps no other scriptural portion more deserving of our attention, for it not only captures the very essence of Christ's character, but points the reader toward God and the assimilation of His person.

In addition, this chapter will spend a good amount of time examining the proper and improper use of the tongue. There are at least three reasons why: (1) within the body of believers, there is nothing quite so potentially damaging as the tongue, (2) at the same time, there are few things more capable of uplifting, sustaining and edifying, and (3) there are few ways that more effectively measure how "Christ-like" we have become than when we examine the way we use our tongues in light of the scriptural model.

Searching for truth in the shadows
Grace hugs the line of despair
Voices are heard from the darkness
Lost souls go forth without care

Silence the noise not the music
Rest in the way of the sane
Light taps the minds of the chosen
Questioning hearts start to wane

Mysteries fade into stories
Desolate peaks disappear
Depths of great torrent are vanquished
New currents carry the fear

Dawn brings what few seem to harvest
New songs are heard through the night
Dragons are slain in the battle
Spirits rejoice in their flight
P. L. Engstrom

CHAPTER FOUR
The State of Salvation

The Christ hymn found in Philippians 2 is at once both inspirational and intimidating. In fact, it is beyond intimidating as it presents a seemingly impossible challenge to personify the character of Jesus Christ. An appropriate reaction to this hymn's message encompasses a sense of both awe and inadequacy.

No portion of Scripture more adequately depicts the impeccable character of Christ. At the same time, no scriptural portion more clearly communicates the mandate concerning the assimilation of that character--"Have [Christ's] mind among yourselves" (Phil 2:5).

Once Jesus Christ is accepted as Savior, the challenge that remains is an appropriation of His character. This is, after all, the whole point of the New Testament beyond its attempt to present Jesus as Savior.

Washing The Various Feet

Jesus Christ is the ultimate model for moral action. In John 13, for example, we find Jesus, not overwhelmed with anxiety regarding any one of a vast variety of personal difficulties, but instead, overcome by the compassion and concern for others which epitomize His person. Like Philippians 2, John 13 captures the essential part of Christ's prototypical character. Note especially the emphasized phrases, as they serve to remind us of the great struggles Jesus was facing.

> Now before the feast of the Passover, *when Jesus knew that his hour had come to depart out of this world to the Father,* having loved his own who were in the world, he loved them to the end. And during supper, *when the devil had already put it into the heart of Judas Iscariot,* Simon's son, to betray him, Jesus, knowing that the Father had given all things into his hands, and that he had come from God and was going to God, rose from supper, laid aside his garments, and girded himself with a towel (John 13:1-4).

Clearly, Jesus had many things on His mind, not the least of which were the mode of His imminent departure from this world and the betrayal by one of His closest friends and companions. He could have easily been consumed with these thoughts but instead, His garments, which were certainly a symbol of His own selfish concerns, were "laid aside." Jesus' concern for self was displaced by His concern for others. In an hour of what could easily be unyielding desperation, Jesus focused His energies on the needs of others.

> Then he poured water into a basin, and began to wash the disciples' feet, and to wipe them with the towel with which he was girded. He came to Simon Peter; and Peter said to him, "Lord, do you wash my feet?" Jesus answered him, "What I am doing you do not know now, but afterward you will understand." Peter said to him, "You shall never wash my feet." Jesus answered him, "If I do not wash you, you have no part in me." Simon Peter said to him "Lord, not my feet only but also my hands and my head!" (John 13:5-9).

The teaching of this scene in the upper room occurs at three different levels. The first lesson is found in the overt acts and words of Jesus, the second in the somewhat cryptic interchange between Jesus and Peter and the third as the reader is reminded of Judas Iscariot being a background witness to these proceedings.

To comprehend the first teaching, we need only be reminded that it was customary hospitality for hosts to provide their guests with water for their feet. However, the hosts provided only the opportunity; the guests were responsible for washing their own feet. Not even the Jewish slaves were required to perform such a demeaning, lowly task. In fact, they were protected by law from such duty.

Occasionally, as a sign of love and devotion, disciples would provide this service to their teacher or rabbi. However, the teacher would never perform such a task on his students. Jesus did so that His disciples might visually understand how they are to treat and respect and love one another. Jesus never resorted to mere words to express a point; He taught by illustration and more importantly, by example.

> When he had washed their feet, and taken his garments, and resumed his place, he said to them, "Do you know what I have done to you? You call me Teacher and Lord; and you are right, for so I am. If I then, your Lord and Teacher, have washed your feet, *you also ought to wash one another's feet. For I have given you an example, that you also should do as I have done to you* (John 13:12-15).

It is important to note that Jesus' example advocates, even demands that personal pride be displaced by self-humiliation. As Christ's followers, we are to govern in the spiritual sense, acting as moral disinfectants. But, from Jesus' example, we see that we must also act as subservient slaves, attending to the physical well-being of others.

In our world, power and position are largely measured by the amount of money we carry and the number of underlings we boast. In Christ's world, what makes us great is the number of those we serve. In our world, what controls many relationships (or the lack thereof), are things like intolerance, prejudice and narrow-mindedness. These make for virtually impossible impasses when it comes to establishing, sustaining or healing a relationship. In Christ's world, these are replaced with things like acceptance, tolerance and leniency. A sustaining and nurturing spirit of humility always predominates.

> He will not wrangle or cry aloud, nor will any one hear his voice in the streets; he will not break a bruised reed or quench a smoldering wick, till he brings justice to victory (Matt 12:19-20).

In John 13, Jesus' example instructs His followers to be humble before one another. On a deeper, more central level, this scriptural portion foretells and foreshadows Jesus' death on the cross. In the process, the significance and meaning of His death is disclosed. The conversation between Jesus and Peter provides the primary key to this understanding.

> He came to Simon Peter; and Peter said to him, "Lord, do you wash my feet?" Jesus answered him, "If I do not wash you, you have no part in me." Simon Peter said to him, "Lord, not my feet only but also my hands and my head!" Jesus said to him, "He who has bathed does not need to wash, except for his feet, but he is clean all over; and you are clean, but not all of you" (John 13:6-10).

Apart from the actual conversation, the text gives clues as to the meaning of the exchange between Peter and Jesus. In verse 1, for example, we find, "Now before the feast of the Passover, when Jesus knew that his hour had come to depart out of this world . . ." And in verse 3, "Jesus, knowing that the Father had given all things into his hands, and that he had come from God and was going to God . . ."

In both examples, the reader is clued to the fact that Jesus' hour of death was near and that, somehow, the significance of the entire narrative is linked to this realization. However, the dialogue involving Peter and Jesus provides the clearer evidence concerning the imminence of Jesus' death.

The most telling evidence occurs after Peter initially refuses to allow Jesus to wash his feet. Jesus responds by saying, "If I do not wash you, you have no part in me" (verse 8). According to Jesus, the footwashing is so important that without it, a disciple's heritage with

Jesus is lost.   There is no doubt that Jesus is making reference to something other than clean feet.

As with the act of footwashing, so salvation requires both an action and a reaction if it is to be meaningful, having its intended effect. Jesus was willing to wash Peter's feet, but a willingness to receive the washing was also necessary.   Precisely the same is true where salvation is concerned.   Jesus Christ provides the necessary action on the cross, but if people are to benefit from the effects of Christ's death, they must be willing to receive the washing.

As Jesus was going to "wash the disciples' feet" on the cross of Calvary, so were the disciples instructed to bring that salvation to others in the world.   Jesus said, "You also ought to wash one another's feet" (verse 14).   We can only assume that, like the disciples, we are expected to do the same, humbling ourselves before others and bringing them the news that provides eternal life should they choose to accept it.   And let us remember that our obligation is to bring the good news to others.   We are not responsible should they choose to reject it.

A third level of teaching in John 13 occurs regarding the person of Judas Iscariot.   Judas' character becomes more prominent beginning at verse 21, but prior to this, textual clues are offered, helping the reader to focus on Judas, even though he is in the background.   Verse 2, for example, reads, "And during supper, when the devil had already put it into the heart of Judas Iscariot, Simon's son, to betray him . . ." And at the end of the interchange between Jesus and Peter, we find,

> Jesus said to him, "He who has bathed does not need to wash, except for his feet, but he is clean all over; and you are clean, but not all of you. For he knew who was to betray him; that was why he said, "You are not all clean" (John 13:10-11).

There is plenty of indication that the issue of Judas' betrayal is not to be ignored through this footwashing event. And considering what we have discussed concerning the significance of the footwashing, we can only conclude that the inclusion of Judas' betrayal in this scriptural portion is meant to heighten that teaching's significance.

At the time of the footwashing, the disciples were, undoubtedly, unaware of its full significance and were therefore left largely confused by many of Jesus' words. However, after Jesus' death on the cross, this would change. At that time, the disciples would look back on the footwashing, remember the words spoken and be enlightened in a way they could not have been previously. And what would be largely responsible for this would be their new found knowledge of Judas' betrayal. Only then could the full impact of Jesus' teaching be realized. The footwashing had everything to do with forgiveness. Clearly, Jesus knew of the impending betrayal as He washed Judas' feet. It then stands to reason that Jesus was offering forgiveness to the one who would be largely responsible for sending Him to the cross. After Calvary, the disciples would look back on this with tremendous awe. And the constraint placed upon them to "do as Jesus did" would be even more compelling. They would have forever before them a perfect model of humility and forgiveness.

We must not overlook the fact that the intentions of Judas were viewed as reprehensible, even culpable. Jesus clearly treated his intent to sin as he would sin itself. Therefore, we must conclude that acts, in and of themselves, do not delimit what is considered sinful.

Becoming Like The Master

In many ways, John 13 provides us with teaching similar to that found in Philippians 2. Both present Jesus Christ as the model to be followed, then encourage, even command the followers of Jesus to be like Him.

Immediately prior to the Christ-hymn in Philippians 2, the apostle Paul is pleading with the Philippians to be like-minded, caring more for one another than they do themselves.

> So if there is any encouragement in Christ, any incentive of love, any participation in the Spirit, any affection and sympathy, complete my joy by being of the same mind, having the same love, being in full accord and of one mind. Do nothing from selfishness or conceit, but in humility count others better than yourselves. Let each of you look not only to his own interests, but also to the interests of others. (Phil 2:1-4).

Paul does more than offer suggestion. There is an urgent pleading that issues as much from Paul's wisdom concerning community relationships as it does from Paul's responsibility to instruct the church regarding their obligation to love and care for one another. After this pleading, Paul recites the hymn, pointing to Jesus Christ as the example for His people to follow.

> Have this mind among yourselves, which you have in Christ Jesus, who, though he was in the form of God, did not count equality with God a thing to be grasped, but emptied himself, taking the form of a servant, being born in the likeness of men. And being found in human form he humbled himself and became obedient unto death, even death on a cross. Therefore God has highly exalted him and bestowed on him the name which is above every name, that at the name of Jesus every knee should bow, in heaven and on earth and under the earth,

and every tongue confess that Jesus Christ is Lord, to the glory of God the Father (Phil 2:5-11).

It can be observed that the flow of action in this hymn is similar, if not identical to the progression observed in the footwashing event in John 13. In John's gospel, Jesus (1) "laid aside his garments" (John 13:4), (2) "washed his disciples' feet" (John 13:5), (3) "took his garments and resumed his place" (John 13:12), then (4) announced that He was Lord (John 13:13). The same progression occurs in Philippians as Jesus (1) "emptied himself" (Phil 2:7), (2) "humbled himself and became obedient unto death" (Phil 2:8), (3) was "highly exalted" (Phil 2:9), then (4) had His Lordship announced (Phil 2:11). And in both John 13 and Philippians 2, the followers of Jesus are instructed to be like Jesus, following His example given.

Jesus makes the ultimate sacrifice in two different realms. The footwashing demonstrates Jesus' willingness to be completely humble in the earthly sense while His death on the cross, with its accompanying acceptance of sin, portrays a willingness to be completely humble in the spiritual sense. As we saw in chapter one, Moses, like Jesus, was willing to sacrifice himself spiritually, for after the Israelites constructed the golden calf, Moses went before the Lord and said,

"Alas, this people have sinned a great sin; they have made for themselves gods of gold. But now, if thou wilt forgive their sin--and if not, blot me, I pray thee, out of thy book which thou hast written" (Exod 32:31-32).

Moses was not required to give up his soul that others might find forgiveness. And even though he may have been willing, God would not allow an exchange of such magnitude. However, Moses was required to forfeit his inheritance in the Land of Promise.

Apparently, as we saw in chapter one, this forfeiture was the result of his disobedience recorded in Numbers 20. And from this, we learn that disobedience often results in loss. But, what we must also observe is that Moses' status within the community of faith placed him in a position of vulnerability that would not otherwise be present.

Moses' responsibilities were great, as were the demands and expectations placed upon him. Clearly, he was under more pressure than those who simply stood by, waiting to see whether Moses would succeed or fail. Although no acceptable excuse can be offered on Moses' behalf, what can be observed is that Moses' obedience to God made him more susceptible to hardship. What remains true today is that the greater the position of responsibility, the more potential there is for loss.

Moses undoubtedly suffered emotionally throughout his leadership, but more than this was lost. He was forced to give up that for which he had worked for many years, that being the Promised land. After Moses' sin, God offered no concessions, no allowances, no indulgences. In fact, God was probably harder on Moses than He was on those with a lesser ability to influence the lives of others.

Very few in our world are like Moses, willing to sacrifice their eternal destiny that others might find deliverance. And while Paul is not likely teaching that this is expected, he is clearly teaching there must be a willingness to give up a portion of our earthly selves and, if necessary, a portion of our spiritual well-being if it means others will receive benefit.

We need only be reminded of the examples of Moses and Jeremiah to know that this type of sacrifice is not unheard of, nor is it unexpected. Both of these men suffered in countless ways in order that the people of Israel might receive opportunity to be delivered.

It is unfortunate that so many people today see humility and self-sacrifice as weakness. To be sure, they are nothing of the kind. Rather, they are to be likened to a divine signature, one which God's people are expected to write and to re-write in their own lives time and time again.

Nowhere does the Bible teach that followers of God will be exempt from hardship. Where do people get the idea that suffering, whether it be physical or emotional or spiritual, is incompatible with the salvation offered by God? As a matter of fact, as we have seen, the Bible seems to teach the opposite.

According to Philippians 2, a Christian disciple has no choice but to offer humble, self-sacrificing service to others in love. If this kind of attitude and service is not offered, then Christian discipleship, very simply, does not exist.

However, following these examples of Christ in John 13 and Philippians 2 has its positive side, for at the end of this cycle of humiliation, there is exaltation. Unfortunately, it may not be realized until the years of hard work and hardship are over. But for those who endure to the end, there is exaltation, praise and thanksgiving. This must not comprise the motivation of our actions, and indeed, if it does, the actions will not be manifest, but let us always remember, there is reward for those who persevere.

> And Jesus called them to him and said to them, "You know that those who are supposed to rule over the Gentiles lord it over them, and their great men exercise authority over them. But it shall not be so among you; but whoever would be great among you must be your servant, and whoever would be first among you must be slave of all. For the Son of man also came not to be served but to serve, and to give his life as a ransom for many (Mark 10:42-45).

In John 13 and Philippians 2, Jesus ignores His divine character and position, humbling Himself instead to a place of servitude. In both scriptural portions, it is made clear that Jesus' followers are to do the same. And the point is this: If Jesus can leave His place of heavenly glory, descend to earth and perform tasks reserved for the lowliest, most despicable people, then surely His followers can take whatever steps are necessary to become servants to their brothers and sisters.

The humiliation expected of Jesus' followers is comparatively smaller than that of Jesus'. Clearly, the gulf between Christ's throne and Jesus' cross was infinitely greater than the distance between Jesus' followers and the people they are expected to serve. As a matter of fact, the need to "humble oneself" exists only in the imagination; the whole concept of ranking and categorizing people into respective slots of relative worth is an indefensible activity. And the apostle Paul addresses this issue in his first letter to the Corinthians.

This letter was largely occasioned by the Corinthians' lack of spiritual maturity. Concerning this underdevelopment, Paul cites as an indicator the fact that there was widespread disagreement, even argument, as to which leader of the Corinthian church was more effective or more capable than the other.

The people of our day experience the same problem, demonstrated in one way by the sense of elitism that exists within various denominations, as though particular denominational distinctives are correct to the exclusion of all other distinctives. It is truly remarkable how many "Christians" find it difficult to be the least bit tolerant across denominational boundaries, becoming unyielding, even prejudiced against other faith communities.

Issues related to biblical translations, attire, jewelry, the order of service, etc., etc., seem to take precedent over issues of substance which speak to the immortal soul. Christian communities, regardless of their affiliation and distinctives have a tremendous amount of common ground, but often choose to focus on their differences.

In the Corinthian church of Paul's day, the same narrow-minded immaturity was demonstrated. Not unlike that to which we are accustomed in our world, the Corinthians made a contest of the ridiculous. Paul spoke to the problem directly.

> But I, brethren, could not address you as spiritual men, but as men of the flesh, as babes in Christ. I fed you with milk, not solid food; for you were not ready for it; and even yet you are not ready, for you are still of the flesh. For while there is jealousy and strife among you, are you not of the flesh, and behaving like ordinary men? For when one says, "I belong to Paul," and another, "I belong to Apollos," are you not merely men? (1 Cor 3:1-4)

Paul addresses the squabbling factions, but in the process, he makes it clear that no church leader is to be exalted above another. The probable reason is that one person has no more glory in God's eyes than another person. Ranking and quantifying the relative worth of individuals is a ludicrous exercise, having no merit. It betrays a spiritual immaturity to be practiced by those who are self absorbed-- consumed by an involvement in unprofitable exercises inconsistent with the mind of God. For in God's eyes, all are equal.

What has been far too predominant throughout the generations is a contentious, competitive spirit that is good only for prompting argumentation, stirring animosity and provoking feelings of ill-will. For whatever reason, there lies resident within people a predisposition toward proving an opinion, expressing a belief as though there are no other options, and insisting on an attitude consistent with only their perceptions and knowledge. And often times, all of this effort and energy are expended on behalf of that which has no inherent value or significance.

At times, it seems that people speak only to be heard, express themselves only that others might be proven wrong, and initiate controversy only because it is within them to do so. This is exactly what we see in the Corinthian church. Clearly, their hearts were directed away from value-filled projects as they contended among themselves to no significant end.

Indeed, "humbling" ourselves occurs only in the imagination, for God placed people in this world equally. There is no basis for ascribing more worth to one person than another. One may be more intelligent than another in the sense that he has amassed more information in one area or another, but another may be skilled in an area where the "intelligent" person is completely lost. This does not make one more important than the other; it simply illustrates the co-dependence we all share.

> What then is Apollos? What is Paul? Servants through whom you believed, as the Lord assigned to each. I planted, Apollos watered, but God gave the growth. So neither he who plants nor he who waters is anything, but only God who gives the growth. He who plants and he who waters are equal, and each shall receive his wages according to his labor. For we are fellow workers for God; you are God's field, God's building (1 Cor 3:5-9).

As dissimilar as is the amount of distance traveled between Christ and the cross and Jesus' followers and servanthood, the patterns of humiliation are analogous. As Jesus became subservient, so must those who follow Him. And as Jesus' self-humiliation led Him to a place of great exaltation, so are Jesus' followers brought to a place of exaltation and honor. But this never occurs as the result of self-exaltation and pride.

> A dispute also arose among them, which of them was to be regarded as the greatest. And he said to them, "the kings of the Gentiles exercise lordship over them; and those in authority over them are called benefactors. But not so with you; rather let the greatest among you become as the youngest, and the leader as one who serves (Lk 22:24-26).

The "greatest" is the one who is least concerned about reward. The one who will receive the most is the one who is seeking the least. This makes for a very ironic situation in that the person who is considered the "greatest" and is, therefore, the one to receive the grandest reward, is the one who has most effectively transcended the need for it. In other words, the one who is the least interested in receiving recognition or reward is the person who will receive the largest share.

In God's eyes, it is never money or power or social standing that sets one person apart from another, only the spiritual regeneration that occurs through Jesus Christ and the servitude that accompanies it. And here again, there is irony, for, on the one hand, regeneration through Christ makes one great in the spiritual sense, while, on the other hand, that same regeneration compels one to be subservient in the earthly sense.

When a person accepts Christ as Savior, there is a "re-positioning" that occurs in the spiritual realm. This re-positioning can only be viewed as an "advancement" but it is "proven" and "seated" only as that same person humbles himself in the earthly sphere, becoming a servant to those around him. And the way a person responds to that God-given responsibility determines whether there is a reward to be received or a loss to be suffered.

The Consequences Of Failure

Many wonder what is the nature of the reward to be received. But a person who has truly assimilated the character of Jesus Christ will not question the amount or the contour of his reward. Instead, like Moses, that person will be concerned about others, asking that he might be denied the eternity of God that others might gain access.

The person who has become like Christ will never measure the reward he receives. Instead, his attitude will encompass a sense of sufficiency. Therefore, any reward possessed by anyone else, whatever may be the quantity or quality, is something over which to rejoice. There will be no hard feelings, no remorse, no questions of any kind, just a confidence that God has judged and acted appropriately.

However, after rewards are received, there will be much scrutiny, with many questions being asked. But these will emerge from selfish considerations, from the mouths of those who have experienced, not spiritual reward but spiritual loss. And sadly, there will be many who fall into this category.

Specific divine appointments will be unfulfilled, but perhaps more significantly, the general duty to emulate Christ's person will likewise be mishandled by a large number of people. The consequences of such failures can be illustrated in two ways; one by Paul's letter to the Corinthians and the other from the book of Joshua.

In his first letter to the Corinthians, Paul makes reference to the foundation of Jesus Christ upon which all Corinthian church members are built. In other words, beneath them is the salvation afforded by Jesus Christ. But, upon this constant of Jesus Christ lies great variation, for beyond salvation, the Corinthians are responsible as individuals for answering both the general call to be Christ-like and the various specific appointments God has ordained.

> According to the commission of God given to me, like a skilled master builder I laid a foundation, and another man is building upon it. Let each man take care how he builds upon it. For no other foundation can any one lay than that which is laid, which is Jesus Christ (1 Cor 3:10-11).

Paul goes on to speak of the consequences each person faces regarding the relative quality of the work that follows salvation. For some, the work added to their salvation will be consumed by the fire of God; for others, that same fire will refine their work, giving it the eternal significance of which it is deserving.

> Now if any one builds on the foundation with gold, silver, precious stones, wood, hay, stubble--each man's work will become manifest; for the Day will disclose it, because it will be revealed with fire, and the fire will test what sort of work each one has done. If the work which any man has built on the foundation survives, he will receive a reward. If any man's work is burned up, he will suffer loss, though he himself will be saved, but only as through fire (1 Cor 3:12-15).

As already mentioned, every person has an obligation to become like Christ. That statement, more than any other, comprises the heart of this discourse. But beyond this, every person is assigned special tasks or duties, given in accordance with their abilities and circumstances. And whether we like to believe it or not, God will judge His people with regard to how they deal with their responsibilities.

This allows for an infinite number of scenarios, all of which have a life of their own; at the same time, they are inextricably interconnected. Intersections are created as the constant quality of Jesus Christ comes into contact with the ever-shifting unpredictability of humankind. Some build upon their salvation as God intends, satisfying God's expectations while providing benefit to others. Others build that which has no lasting value.

All of this points to an existence that is in a state of fluctuation. For those who mishandle their responsibilities, life may be understood as that which is unpredictable. But for those who work in concert with God's plan, existence is more positively perceived as that which is transitional or progressive.

Life is appropriately defined as that which results from an intersection of both divine and human participation. God ordains both elements to work in unison to provide what is the framework for life. And this is important, because it reminds us that humanity, with all of its variation, produces consequences just as various.

Concerning the fact that both divine and human elements form the framework for reality, Genesis offers some insight. From Genesis, we learn that, from the beginning, God never intended the act of creation to be an exclusively divine one.

> So out of the ground the LORD God formed every beast of the field and every bird of the air, and brought them to the man to see what he would call them; and whatever the man called every living creature, that was its name (Gen 2:19).

Naming the animals and the birds was part of the creative process, and man was allowed to actively participate. No less is true today. As people move and breathe, make decisions and invite consequences, they do so, not only for themselves, but for others as well. The book of Joshua offers illustration.

Before the people of Israel were to battle the city of Jericho, a very clear directive was given to the people regarding the gold and the silver of that city.

> But you, keep yourselves from the things devoted to destruction, lest when you have devoted them you take any of the devoted things and make the camp of Israel a thing for destruction, and bring trouble upon it. But all silver and gold, and vessels of bronze and iron, are sacred to the LORD; they shall go into the treasury of the LORD (Josh 6:18-19).

The directive was given, the Israelites advanced and Jericho was defeated. Having gained victory over such a powerful army, the Israelites were confident when they later approached the comparatively small city of Ai. There was very little concern, especially when the scouting report came back.

> Let not all the people go up, but let about two or three thousand men go up and attack Ai; do not make the whole people toil up there, for they are but few (Josh 7:3).

Joshua agreed with the report and sent only three thousand into battle. But to Joshua's surprise and dismay, his troops were defeated at Ai. While no one so much as broke a sweat at Jericho, thirty-six men lost their lives at Ai. When Joshua inquired of God as to the reason, the answer came,

> Israel has sinned; they have transgressed my covenant which I commanded them; they have taken some of the devoted

things; they have stolen, and lied, and put them among their own stuff. Therefore the people of Israel cannot stand before their enemies; they turn their backs before their enemies, because they have become a thing for destruction. I will be with you no more, unless you destroy the devoted things from among you (Josh 7:11-12).

These are some rather startling words, especially as we read on and find out it was only one man who stole the silver and the gold. And this discovery leads to some very interesting, if not revelatory observations.

First of all, the sin of one man is spoken of as though it is the sin of the entire community. Here, we are reminded of God's perspective that involves, not the individual but the community.

Secondly, God says, "I will be with you no more, unless you destroy the devoted things from among you (verse 12). In other words, no person would benefit from the presence of God until the situation involving the sin of one person was rectified. The act had to be undone to the degree it was capable. In other words, God did not hold only Achan accountable for his sin but the entire body of believers. All were responsible.

This serves to remind us that sin must be undone to the degree we are able to un-do it. If we need to forgive someone, then that must happen. If restitution is possible for a trangression committed, then restitution must be given. We must always do what we are able because an unwilling spirit betrays a lack of concern and/or penitence. And a person cannot be forgiven if that person does not care enough to offer whatever recompense is possible given the circumstances. However, we must also remember something else. If we have done what is humanly possible concerning restitution for our sin, we are then free to move on without guilt or remorse or distraction.

Thirdly, and perhaps most significantly for our discussion, we need to understand the significance of thirty-six men losing their lives, not because of their own sin, but because of the sin of another. Amazingly, the families of thirty-six men were irretrievably affected because one man--one perhaps they did not even know--sinned in the sight of God.

From this story, it becomes clear that the people of God are responsible for one another, that their actions yield consequences, not only for themselves, but for others. Moreover, the relationship of God to the entire community of faith can be, and is, affected by the actions of just one person. This places in perspective the tremendous significance of the individual fulfilling both his general and specific obligations to God.

The people of God are indeed involved in the ongoing creative process of God. Lives are changed in this world, and for that matter, all eternity is potentially re-directed as the result of individual obedience and disobedience. The fate of humanity lies in the hands of those who comprise it.

Given all this, we must ask ourselves if we are doing the work God has assigned us. Are we assimilating the character of Christ or becoming more and more a part of the mediocrity that surrounds us? Are we accomplishing the specific appointments divinely mandated or are we allowing spiritual ambivalence to circumvent our efforts?

While the general purpose and plan of God is unchanging and irrepressible, the individuals used to accomplish that plan and purpose are anything but predictable. The human part of the equation is never vanquished and it only stands to reason that humanity itself is affected by the potential variation of its participants.

Practicing The Royal Law

The apostle Paul and James have very similar concerns. Like the apostle Paul, James has no time for those who make determinations and judgments based upon frivolous surface issues such as money, clothing and social standing. James knows this leads, among other things, to preferential treatment which leads to misunderstandings. And when partiality is shown, the real concerns of God are misrepresented.

> My brethren, show no partiality as you hold the faith of our Lord Jesus Christ, the Lord of glory. For if a man with gold rings and in fine clothing comes into your assembly, and a poor man in shabby clothing also comes in, and you pay attention to the one who wears the fine clothing and say, "Have a seat here, please," while you say to the poor man, "Stand there," or, "Sit at my feet," have you not made distinctions among yourselves, and become judges with evil thoughts? (James 2:1-4)

Like Paul, James teaches the primacy of relationships, how the treatment of others is to take precedent over our own well-being. According to James, a new law is to be practiced, the law inaugurated by the person of Jesus Christ.

> If you really fulfil the royal law, according to the scripture, "You shall love your neighbor as yourself," you do well. But if you show partiality, you commit sin, and are convicted by the law as transgressors (James 2:8-9).

If the Royal Law is truly being practiced, then there are no disagreements, no hurt feelings and no need to be correct at the expense of someone else's dignity. There is only the humility and the meekness which come forth as a person encounters and subsequently assimilates the person of Christ.

> Who is wise and understanding among you? By his good life let him show his works in the meekness of wisdom. But if you have bitter jealousy and selfish ambition in your hearts, do not boast and be false to the truth. This wisdom is not such as comes down from above, but is earthly, unspiritual, devilish. For where jealousy and selfish ambition exist, there will be disorder and every vile practice (James 3:13-16).

James is as direct as the apostle Paul when it comes to relationships. If there is selfishness and arrogance, no good will result. As a matter of fact, because it is "earthly, unspiritual, devilish," it is the breeding ground for disharmony and discord. According to James, the person who has properly assimilated the character of Christ will be vastly different.

> But the wisdom from above is first pure, then peaceable, gentle, open to reason, full of mercy and good fruits, without uncertainty or insincerity. And the harvest of righteousness is sown in peace by those who make peace (James 3:17-18).

For Christians, the emphasis must always be on the other person, never on the self. Egocentric motives and concerns have no place in the life of a person who has assimilated Christ.

James spends a good deal of time addressing practical matters. Whereas this has been a point of confusion for some, James' emphasis follows the teachings of Jesus Christ and the apostle Paul to the letter. At no time does James invalidate the importance or the necessity of faith; he teaches from the context of faith, giving instruction in keeping with the rest of the New Testament.

For James, a relationship with Christ must be demonstrable. It must manifest itself by good works, or it possesses no earthly good.

> What does it profit, my brethren, if a man says he has faith but has not works? Can his faith save him? If a brother or sister is ill-clad and in lack of daily food, and one of you says to them, "Go in peace, be warmed and filled," without giving them the things needed for the body, what does it profit? So faith by itself, if it has no works, is dead (James 2:14-17).

Jesus Himself spoke of the care we must offer one another, and did so in the context of judgment. He did not speak of it as though it were a side issue; He spoke of providing for one another as though it were the central issue. As we have seen, with Christianity, it is impossible to get away from relationships. By our relationships we shall be judged unworthy and by our relationships, we shall be vindicated.

> "When the Son of man comes in his glory, and all the angels with him, then he will sit on his glorious throne. Before him will be gathered all the nations, and he will separate them one from another as a shepherd separates the sheep from the goats, and he will place the sheep at his right hand, but the goats at the left. Then the King will say to those at his right hand, `Come, O Blessed of my Father, inherit the kingdom prepared for you from the foundation of the world; for I was hungry and you gave me food, I was thirsty and you gave me drink, I was a stranger and you welcomed me, I was naked and you clothed me, I was sick and you visited me, I was in prison and you

came to me.' Then the righteous will answer him, `Lord, when did we see thee hungry and feed thee, or thirsty and give thee drink? And when did we see thee a stranger and welcome thee, or naked and clothe thee? And when did we see thee sick or in prison and visit thee?' And the King will answer them, `Truly, I say to you, as you did it to one of the least of these my brethren, you did it to me.' Then he will say to those at his left hand, "Depart from me, you cursed, into the eternal fire prepared for the devil and his angels; for I was hungry and you gave me no food, I was thirsty and you gave me no drink, I was a stranger and you did not welcome me, naked and you did not clothe me, sick and in prison and you did not visit me.' Then they also will answer, `Lord, when did we see thee hungry or thirsty or a stranger or naked or sick or in prison, and did not minister to thee?' Then he will answer them, `Truly, I say to you, as you did it not to one of the least of these, you did it not to me.' And they will go away into eternal punishment, but the righteous into eternal life" (Matt 25:31-46).

Charting Your Progress

As we have already discussed, the book of James insists on a faith that is demonstrable; without practical manifestation, faith is without both value and substance, possessing no earthly good. And, as seen throughout these chapters, if there is no contribution to the well-being of others, then no evidence exists for a relationship with God.

James can be looked upon as a series of tests, written for the person who professes salvation through faith in Jesus Christ. Words can be meaningful, but James' letter provokes a person to examine the sum and substance of that profession. In other words, does that profession of faith provide any demonstrable verification?

Test One

James opens his epistle with an address to those who are suffering because of their Christianity. This is not surprising given that the letter is written specifically to Jews dispersed by persecution (James 1:1). But that is not to say James' words are not directly applicable to Christians of our generation.

James says a Christian should respond to trial with rejoicing because of the many benefits which accompany those trials (James 1:2-4). Clearly, such a response is only possible by those who are spiritually mature. To those who have earthly immaturity, such a response to trials and suffering seems preposterous.

Discussed briefly in the last chapter, James teaches the essential and advantageous nature of trial and temptation. That difficulties bring benefit should come as no surprise, for regardless of the discomfort involved in suffering, a person becomes stronger only when that person is confronted by opposition. The rejoicing comes, not because a person experiences hardship but because the difficulties "produce steadfastness" (James 1:3). And that steadfastness, having its full effect, makes a person "full and complete, lacking in nothing" (James 1:4).

In a somewhat strange but scripturally verifiable way, trial and suffering are necessary antecedents to what James terms the "crown of life" (James 1:12). According to Paul in his letter to the Philippians, it was only after a willingness to humble Himself that Jesus became exalted to a place more prominent that any other (Phil 2:8-11). And according to James, the same holds true for Jesus' followers.

> Blessed is the man who endures trial, for when he has stood the test he will receive the crown of life which God has promised to those who love him (James 1:12).

Concerning trials, there are two conclusions to which we are inevitably led by Scriptures: (1) for the Christian person, trials are considered to be a part of everyday existence; at no time are we led to believe otherwise, and (2) the "crown of life" is awarded to those who persevere through the sufferings. Now, whether or not those sufferings are mandatory is debatable, but looking to the biblical characters as our example, diffculties are, at the very least, unavoidable; at the very most, they are indispensable to the process of becoming.

Test Two

If a person is truly faith-filled, the word of the Lord will not only be heard, but accomplished.

> But be doers of the word, and not hearers only, deceiving yourselves. For if any one is a hearer of the word and not a doer, he is like a man who observes his natural face in a mirror; for he observes himself and goes away and at once forgets what he was like. But he who looks into the perfect law, the law of liberty, and perseveres, being no hearer that forgets but a doer that acts, he shall be blessed in his doing (James 1:22-25).

Before we expound on these four verses, it is important to point out that the verse immediately preceding these four offers an indispensable condition for accomplishing what James instructs. This prerequisite has everything to do with the personal decision to lay aside the old way of life in readiness for the new. James writes very clearly concerning this.

> Therefore put away all filthiness and rank growth of wickedness and receive with meekness the implanted word, which is able to save your souls (James 1:21).

Reminiscent of Colossians 2, James instructs his readers to lay aside the old self and be receptive toward and desirous of the new. For only under these conditions can a person become something other than a passive hearer.

Christianity cannot be defined as passive inactivity. It is something that requires expression and involvement. It can be nothing else. While it is true the person who chooses not to express his Christianity is more likely to avoid controversy and loss of self, it is that same lack of involvement that effectively brings a halt to that person's quest for the crown of life. In fact, any kind of positive recognition by God is not possible apart from a Christianity that is characterized by both involvement and expression.

James says that a hearer of the word is like a person who "observes his natural face in the mirror and goes away and at once forgets what he was like" (James 1:23-24). What this means is that the person who merely hears the word is a person who does not look into its depth. Obviously, that person does not intend to apply that word to his life.

God's Word is meant to be life-changing, not just informational. God expects His words to take root and to grow, effecting change in every aspect of a person's life. Only when God's word has become interconnected with a person's fundamental character can that person become a "doer" of God's word, not just a listener. As we have seen in countless ways, there must be an inner transformation.

Test Three

According to James, a Christian person will have a perspective encompassing a concern that goes beyond this earth. This is not something that can be taught or explained with any degree of accuracy, for it is that which envelopes a person from within.

James teaches that the relative worth of individuals must not be measured by financial position or social standing. The Christian perspective always has as its focus the eternal soul rather than the human exterior.

> My brethren, show no partiality as you hold the faith of our Lord Jesus Christ, the Lord of glory. For if a man with gold rings and in fine clothing comes into your assembly, and a poor man in shabby clothing also comes in, and you pay attention to the one who wears the fine clothing and say, "Have a seat here, please," while you say to the poor man, "Stand there," or, "Sit at my feet," have you not made distinctions among yourselves, and become judges with evil thoughts? (James 1:1-4)

James addresses people who have yet to transcend the tendency to surround themselves with people who may be helpful to them. In other words, selfish considerations yet predominate their thinking; there remains an egocentricity that not only belies spiritual immaturity, but prevents these people from conducting God's business as Christ would have them. Apparently, they are more concerned about their own earthly increase than they are the spiritual gain of others. And for those more concerned about earthly riches than spiritual blessing, there is warning that James gives.

> Come now, you rich, weep and howl for the miseries that are
> coming upon you. Your riches have rotted and your garments
> are moth-eaten. Your gold and silver have rusted, and their
> rust will be evidence against you and will eat your flesh like fire
> (James 5:1-3).

James offers, not only instruction, but warning. The person who
works to build up his earthly existence and ignores his spiritual
development will be sadly disappointed in the end. The earthly
treasures are temporary and fleeting while the spiritual self continues
into eternity. Interestingly enough, we are left with the impression
throughout Scriptures that spiritual development has everything to do
with the earthly realm, as though it is our testing ground. As we saw
from 1 Corinthians, eternal loss is suffered when a person's earthly
existence does not yield the spiritual fruits of which it is capable.

As to a Christian's attitude toward this earthly realm, Peter
addresses this issue in his first epistle, making it clear that there is to be
no bonding between this world and those who accept Jesus Christ as
Savior. There is to be a clear separation between the former life apart
from Christ and the present life with Him. Activities change, loyalties
differ and even places of residence shift.

> But you are a chosen race, a royal priesthood, a holy nation,
> God's own people, that you may declare the wonderful deeds
> of him who called you out of darkness into his marvelous light.
> Once you were no people but now you are God's people; once
> you had not received mercy but now you have received mercy.
> Beloved, I beseech you as aliens and exiles to abstain from the
> passions of the flesh that wage war against your soul (1 Pet
> 2:9-11).

Like James, Peter tells his readers that their new way of life with Jesus Christ is conditional upon their decision to lay aside old habits associated with the flesh. These ways do not simply make it more difficult to live as Jesus Christ instructs, but they "wage war" against the very soul, that which comprises a person's very essence.

Test Four

A large portion of James' epistle speaks about the tongue. And without question, the person who is transformed into the image of Christ is one whose speech reflects that transformation.

James does not underestimate the power of the tongue saying,

> [I]t is a fire. The tongue is an unrighteous world among our members, staining the whole body, setting on fire the cycle of nature, and set on fire by hell. For every kind of beast and bird, of reptile and sea creature, can be tamed and has been tamed by humankind, but no human being can tame the tongue--a restless evil, full of deadly poison (James 3:6-8).

When the worlds were created, humankind was given dominion over all living things, over the birds of the sky, the fish in the sea, and the animals which were on the face of the ground. Apparently, man also had dominion over himself. But after the fall, this all changed. Man lost some of his control over the creatures of the world, but also lost dominion over himself. No longer was humankind the master of his own house.

This can be seen in many different ways but perhaps the clearest demonstration is found in the tongue, for the tongue can no longer be trusted. This is no small matter given that the tongue defiles the entire personality and sets on fire the whole course of life. It is a "restless evil, full of deadly poison" (James 3:8).

Obviously, the tongue wields a great deal of power, able to direct the course of an individual's life. But beyond this, many other lives can also be affected, both to their advantage and to their detriment.

Words are powerful because what is spoken is a direct reflection of what is felt. No matter how many times a person says, "I really did not mean to say that," it is too late. Words, even though they are spoken in the heat of the moment, cannot be retrieved. The words of a person are a reflection of thought, feeling and attitude.

One of the things that makes the tongue so "ungodly" is the inconsistency associated with it. It is able to bring great harm to a person, making that person feel depressed and ashamed. However, that same tongue is able to uplift, sustain and cause a person to rejoice greatly. That same tongue, rightly exercised, is able to bring a person into the very presence of God.

Given the fact that the tongue is able to both tear down and lift up, it is no wonder some people have become so cynical and suspicious, distrusting every word that comes from a person's mouth. And in one sense, they cannot be blamed, for it is true that the same tongue can at one moment, bless God, while in the next moment, curse humankind. We have all experienced firsthand how words are flowery and sweet before a particular person's face, but take that person out of the picture and the same tongue produces a whole different vocabulary.

There is no more accurate test of Christ-likeness than to examine the way we use our tongues. Ideally speaking, words will be used always for blessing, never for cursing; words will always yield that which is fresh, never that which is bitter. A manifestation of such idealism is rare, but every Christian should be working with diligence to move always closer to that ideal. If there is such progression, then that person does well.

As it has been said elsewhere in this discourse, there is no challenge in finding fault, no difficulty in pointing out error. Anyone can practice these and subsequently publicize their findings. What is much more difficult is to build up, uplift, sustain, inspire and strengthen. And our words are capable of doing all of these and more, if we will only allow that Christ portion of ourselves to surface.

Having the ability to speak brings with it tremendous responsibility. The words from our mouths can be sinful themselves, but they can also arouse sin in others. All the potential evil within each one of us can find expression by, and be aroused by the tongue. On the other hand, the tongue can arouse all that is good within people. Our words can bring the very best to life, not only in ourselves, but in others.

> For every kind of beast and bird, of reptile and sea creature, can be tamed and has been tamed by humankind, but no human being can tame the tongue--a restless evil, full of deadly poison. With it we bless the Lord and Father, and with it we curse men, who are made in the likeness of God. From the same mouth come blessing and cursing. My brethren, this ought not to be so (James 3:7-10).

James places much importance in the control of the tongue, going so far as to say it is a necessary part of wisdom. Immediately after James addresses the issue of the tongue he writes,

> Who is wise and understanding among you? By his good life let him show his works in the meekness of wisdom" (James 3:13).

These words challenge those who profess to be wise, but are not. And it is by their conduct they have proven they have not grasped the true character of wisdom.

The genuine Christian will always exhibit wisdom by the kind of life he lives, especially where human relationships are concerned. He will control his tongue and shun strife and controversy. To the Hebrew mind, this is what comprises true wisdom; true wisdom is that which is moral rather than intellectual. And for James, the control of the tongue comprises an essential part of morality.

The Use Of The Tongue

Psalm 34 carries our discussion further in that it refers to the words people speak as being a measure of their righteousness; not just righteousness as it is perceived by other people, but righteousness as it is measured by the mind of God.

The psalmist begins by declaring his resolute stance to offer praise unto the Lord. The psalmist has obviously been delivered from some difficulty, and as he offers what is essentially a vow to continually thank God for that deliverance, he invites others to do two things: (1) hear what the Lord has done on the psalmist's behalf, and (2) respond by praising God, not only because of what He has done for the 34th psalmist, but because of the deliverance God offers to everyone who calls upon His name.

> I will bless the Lord at all times; his praise shall continually be in my mouth. My soul makes its boast in the LORD; let the afflicted hear and be glad. O magnify the LORD with me, and let us exalt his name together! I sought the LORD, and he answered me, and delivered me from all my fears. Look to him, and be radiant; so your faces shall never be ashamed. This

poor man cried, and the LORD heard him, and saved him out of all his troubles (Ps 34:1-6).

One of the things most appealing about the psalms in general is their timelessness. Christians through the centuries have turned to the psalms as a source of guidance and inspiration. God-fearing people across the generations are able to do so because few specifics are given regarding the circumstances involved in the various deliverances. As a result, history is transcended as people of God pour out their hearts in response to the Lord's activity in their lives. Psalm 34 is no exception.

That Psalm 34 is a hymn of deliverance can hardly be overlooked but let us not miss the important message it offers concerning the use of the tongue. First of all, it is clear the psalmist intends to use his words to praise God. In fact, his words will be such that God's praise will always be heard with great clarity. Secondly, the psalmist's words are used to stimulate other hearts to praise God for His wondrous acts, to view God as the one who is both source and resource.

Verses 7-10 offer instruction related to the "fear" of the Lord. And this "fear" is significant for our discussion.

The angel of the LORD encamps around those who fear him, and delivers them. O taste and see that the LORD is good! Happy is the man who takes refuge in him! O fear the LORD, you his saints, for those who fear him have no want! The young lions suffer want and hunger; but those who seek the LORD lack no good thing (Ps 34:7-10).

Clearly, the Lord's presence is with those who "fear" Him. And according to the psalmist, God's presence brings a person three things: (1) deliverance, (2) no want of anything, and (3) no lack of any good thing.

"Fear" can refer to many things in the Old Testament: (1) the emotion of fear (Deut 5:5), (2) an anticipation of evil (Gen 31:31), (3) a feeling of reverance or awe (Ps 112:1), (4) righteous, appropriate behavior (Deut 17:19), and (5) formalized worship (2 Kgs 17:32-34).

In Psalm 34, the usage is likely related to the reverance and awe a person has towards God when these feelings are appropriately translated into everyday, righteous behavior.   This is made clear in verses 11 through 14 when the psalmist stops to make sure his listeners know what is the definition of the fear of the Lord.

> Come, O sons, listen to me, I will teach you the fear of the LORD.   What man is there who desires life, and covets many days, that he may enjoy good?   Keep your tongue from evil, and your lips from speaking deceit.   Depart from evil, and do good;   seek peace, and pursue it (Ps 34:11-14).

In other words, fearing God and living properly with other people are ideas so closely related as to be virtually synonymous. According to the psalmist, the person who fears the Lord is one who uses his tongue properly and pursues peaceful relationships with those around him.

This teaching is far from unprecedented in Scripture.   For example, in the nineteenth chapter of Leviticus, there is much instruction related to the proper treatment of neighbor.   In verse 14, such treatment is unmistakably paralleled with fearing the Lord. "You shall not curse the deaf or put a stumbling block before the blind, but you shall fear your God" (Lev 19:14).   In other words, fearing God is the same as doing well before your neighbor.

As we look to the 34th psalmist's discussion concerning the "fear" of the Lord, we must not overlook the movement related to the use of the tongue.   At first, the psalmist's lips were used to praise God;

he then invites others to join in verbal celebration of the Lord's deliverance. When the psalmist then gives instruction as to the practical response to the Lord's deliverance, there is the clear directive to use the tongue appropriately where other people are concerned.

According to the psalmist, it is not enough for us to praise God and to use our mouths in celebration of His good works; we must also use our tongues in a way that is right and proper before one another. Giving God the kind of reverance of which He is deserving works in direct association with the way we conduct ourselves on this earth with one another. The psalmist teaches that only then does God continue to listen to the cries of His people and offer deliverance to them when they call upon His name.

> The eyes of the Lord are toward the righteous, and his ears toward their cry. The face of the LORD is against evildoers, to cut off the remembrance of them from the earth. When the righteous cry for help, the LORD hears, and delivers them out of all their troubles (Ps 34:15-17).

God weighs the righteousness of His people, even going so far as to measure their devotion to Him by the way they conduct themselves before one another. Righteousness itself is evaluated, even quantified, as people act with and react to one another. And people's actions are directly related to God's actions; from the actions of His people, God determines whether redemption is offered or denied as He appraises behaviors and attitudes.

> Many are the afflictions of the righteous; but the LORD delivers him out of them all. He keeps all his bones; not one of them is broken. Evil shall slay the wicked; and those who hate the righteous will be condemned. The LORD redeems the life

of his servants; none of those who take refuge in him will be condemned (Ps 34:19-22).

Like James, the 34th psalmist insists on a faith in God that has practical value. The psalmist thinks more in terms of "fearing" God, but the teaching remains the same. The person of faith is one whose relationship with God manifests itself with earthly behavior consistent with the mind of God. Only then is the relationship with God "proven" and only then do God's blessings continue to fall.

And I saw no temple in the city, for its temple is the Lord God the Almighty and the Lamb. And the city has no need of sun or moon to shine upon it, for the glory of God is its light, and its lamp is the Lamb. By its light shall the nations walk; and the kings of the earth shall bring their glory into it, and its gates shall never be shut by day--and there shall be no night there; they shall bring into it the glory and the honor of the nations. But nothing unclean shall enter it, nor any one who practices abomination or falsehood, but only those who are written in the Lamb's book of life (Rev 21:22-27).

CHAPTER FIVE
The Practical Demonstration

A list of do's and don'ts is one of the last things the Bible is. Yet, many people, for whatever reason, insist on reducing God's Word to this level. When the Scriptures are brought to a place where they primarily provide "correct" and "incorrect" behavior, the Bible's depth and insight are significantly diminished; what is meant to be applicable across an endless variety of circumstances and contexts, is now some person's or group's subjective measurement of righteousness.

What this inevitably creates is a situation where a person's actions or activities do not "measure up." And when this occurs, that person is branded as being "unrighteous," "unspiritual," and therefore, "unsaved."

I propose that the Bible teaches condemnation, but not of those who do not measure up to some group's expectations, but of those who create the burdensome yokes and even worse, doing so in the name of righteousness. Speaking of the Pharisees, Jesus said,

> [S]o practice and observe whatever they tell you, but not what they do; for they preach, but do not practice. They bind heavy burdens, hard to bear, and lay them on men's shoulders; but they themselves will not move them with their finger (Matt 23:3-4).

The Bible speaks of inner cleansing and spiritual renewal, not a formally concocted array of behaviors designed to convince others and self of "holiness." Righteousness is internal, and therefore, must come from the heart.

> Woe to you, scribes and Pharisees, hypocrites! for you cleanse the outside of the cup and of the plate, but inside they are full of extortion and rapacity. You blind Pharisee! first cleanse the inside of the cup and of the plate, that the outside also may be clean. Woe to you, scribes and Pharisees, hypocrites! for you are like whitewashed tombs, which outwardly appear beautiful, but within they are full of dead men's bones and all uncleanness. So you also outwardly appear righteous to men, but within you are full of hypocrisy and iniquity (Matt 23:25-28).

Lists of "right" and "wrong" behavior are very self-serving, often created that people might have demonstrable evidence that they lead a "god-like" existence. In reality, they are in place for those who are weak and uncertain, for those who are more interested in impressing others than they are their commitment towards, and faith in God.

I have said what I have about lists that the remainder of this chapter be not mistaken for a burdensome pattern of actions at which any person might become quite practiced, even those who know nothing of God. As a matter of fact, these final thoughts have absolutely nothing to do with how we should perceive the actions of others, or how the other people of this world should be or act; these final thoughts have everything to do with our own attitudes, our own thoughts, our own characteristics. For herein lies salvation: not the judgment and discernment of others, but the examination and subsequent transformation of ourselves.

These final thoughts are but one person's perception of what God's Word teaches concerning the continual pursuit of salvation. No reasonable person would argue that the Bible requires application and that is precisely what this final chapter is: an attempt to summarize in very practical terms what the previous four chapters have drawn directly from Scriptures.

Be Less Reactive

Generally speaking, people lack a proper amount of control. They respond to the moment without giving themselves an opportunity to ponder the various alternatives and potential consequences of their words, actions and reactions. Consequently, their words, spoken in the heat of the moment, are later regretted. And their reactions, thoughtlessly and impetuously displayed, are indelibly etched as permanent impressions in the minds of those who witnessed them.

When suddenly faced with an unnerving or otherwise unexpected situation, often times, our first thoughts are for ourselves. A defensive posture is taken with the accompanying determination to either save face or to, simply, be "in the right." Consequently, there are sudden outbursts of anger with the accompanying words that are much more bountiful than they are thought-filled.

When Moses struck the rock in Numbers 20, he was clearly more concerned about his own agenda than he was God's. By this time, the people of Israel had tried Moses' patience to the breaking point. Likewise, the people of Israel had become less tolerant of Moses as the Exodus version of the incident reveals.

> [B]ut there was no water for the people to drink. Therefore the people found fault with Moses, and said, "Give us water to drink." And Moses said to them, "Why do you find fault with me? Why do you put the LORD to the proof?" But the people thirsted there for water, and the people murmured against Moses, and said, "Why did you bring us up out of Egypt, to kill us and our children and our cattle with thirst?" (Exod 17:1-3)

The only person in this story who maintained his composure, who continued to position His concerns outside his own personal perimeter, was the Lord. The complaints of the people were aimed largely at the Lord, but God showed no signs of anger. Instead, He gave Moses instructions that would provide the people with physical well-being.

> Take the rod, and assemble the congregation, you and Aaron your brother, and tell the rock before their eyes to yield its water; so you shall bring water out of the rock for them; so you shall give drink to the congregation and their cattle (Num 20:8-9).

Moses received simple instructions, but because of his anger and his frustration, spoke words which were inappropriate and performed actions which were uncalled for.

> And Moses and Aaron gathered the assembly together before the rock, and he said to them, "Hear now, you rebels; shall we bring forth water for you out of this rock?" And Moses lifted up his hand and struck the rock with his rod twice; and water came forth abundantly, and the congregation drank, and their cattle (Num 20:10-11).

Moses took advantage of the opportunity to vent his frustrations by chastising the people of God. God nourishes the people, but does not neglect to punish Moses for his actions.

Paul tells us in his first epistle to the Corinthians that love is both patient and kind (1 Cor 13:4). And it is not by accident that these words occur in the same verse, for these displays of "godliness" often have opportunity to manifest themselves simultaneously. The apostle Paul also instructed the Corinthians not to act unbecomingly or to be easily provoked (1 Cor 13:5).

Even though Moses may have had "good reason" to be upset with the people of Israel, God allowed no excuses for his behavior. Regardless of the circumstances and previous treatment Moses had received from the people, Moses was required to be both patient and kind.

The Christians of this world must take the initiative to act in a Christ-like manner regardless of how they are being treated themselves. The Bible does not instruct the followers of Christ to be patient only when being treated fairly, or to be kind only when kindness is offered. Christ-like patience and control must be practiced . . . period. There is no scriptural room for outbursts, whether they be physical or emotional; there is no allowance, under any circumstances, for an uncontrolled, ill-conceived use of the tongue.

Be More Respectful

When God was with Adam and Eve in the garden of Eden, He spoke to them in gentle terms, involved them in his creative activities, and gave them freedom to be whomever they wished to be. God made clear to them His expectations and preferences, but left open the opportunity for them to become something different.

God was nothing if not respectful to His creation, even after they disappointed Him with their disobedience. Knowing full well Adam and Eve had no adequate excuse for their disobedient behavior, God asked questions, allowing them an opportunity to explain.

> And they heard the sound of the LORD God walking in the garden in the cool of the day, and the man and his wife hid themselves from the presence of the LORD God among the trees of the garden. But the LORD God called to the man, and said to him, "Where are you?" And he said, "I heard the sound of thee in the garden, and I was afraid, because I was naked; and I hid myself." He said, "Who told you that you were naked? Have you eaten of the tree of which I commanded you not to eat?" The man said, "The woman whom thou gavest to be with me, she gave me fruit of the tree, and I ate." Then the LORD God said to the woman, "What is this that you have done?" The woman said, "The serpent beguiled me, and I ate" (Gen 3:8-13).

As discussed previously, there were ramifications of this disobedience affecting all of humankind, but God continued to be respectful, even after Adam and Eve were banished from the garden.

God remained respectful to Adam and Eve, issuing their punishment with kindness. And concerning God's relationship with Adam and Eve beyond this point, God continued to instruct them with gentleness, always remaining an active, nurturing part of their lives.

God is a difficult example to follow, but often times, scriptural characters simply do not make for good role models. When it comes to having loving respect, even for those who have disappointed and rejected us, God is clearly the model for us to follow.

Through His prophet Hosea, God announced judgment upon His people, but even as the words were being spoken, the agony God was experiencing shines through with tremendous clarity.

> How can I give you up, O Ephraim! How can I hand you over, O Israel! How can I make you like Admah! How can I treat you like Zeboiim! My heart recoils within me, my compassion grows warm and tender (Hos 11:8).

Though Israel's sin had to be judged because of God's holiness, God was not required to enjoy it, and clearly, He did not. This passage from Hosea testifies not only of God's love for His people, but of the respect He continues to offer them, even when they are continually and grossly disobedient. At no time does God begin to treat his people as though they are less than important.

And, according to Jesus, our respect for others must not be predicated upon the amount of respect we receive. Quite the contrary.

> "You have heard that it was said to the men of old, `You shall not kill; and whoever kills shall be liable to judgment.' But I say to you that every one who is angry with his brother shall be liable to judgment; whoever insults his brother shall be liable to

the council, and whoever says, `You fool!' shall be liable to the hell of fire" (Matt 5:21-22).

Interestingly enough, those who claim the Bible is to be taken "literally" normally allow these verses from Matthew to be translated as "figures of speech," conscious exaggeration used by the author to make a point. This kind of interpretation waters down, even befouls the instruction Jesus is giving, that being the command to respect one another.

It makes no difference if we are familiar with the person, or if the person has cast dispersions on our character. According to the clear teaching of Jesus Christ, what must remain is our respect for that person. Why? Because that person is an eternal soul, one who is in danger of God's judgment, one who is just as important to God as we are. No one person has more significance in God's sight than another.

> "You have heard that it was said, `An eye for an eye and a tooth for a tooth.' But I say to you, Do not resist one who is evil. But if any one strikes you on the right cheek, turn to him the other also; and if any one would sue you and take your coat, let him have your cloak as well; and if any one forces you to go one mile, go with him two miles" (Matt 5:38-41).

Again, Jesus is not using hyperbole. He is serious. We are commanded to respect one another, even if we ourselves are being disrespected. Jesus makes Himself even more clear regarding this point.

> "You have heard that it was said, `You shall love your neighbor and hate your enemy.' But I say to you, Love your enemies and pray for those who persecute you, so that you

may be sons of your Father who is in heaven; for he makes his sun rise on the evil and on the good, and sends rain on the just and on the unjust. For if you love those who love you, what reward have you? Do not even the tax collectors do the same? And if you salute only your brethren, what more are you doing than others? Do not even the Gentiles do the same? You, therefore, must be perfect, as your heavenly Father is perfect" (Matt 5:43-48).

The expectation of perfection is seen again, as it was in our discussion of the first chapter of 2 Peter. According to Jesus, we are to be perfect, "as your heavenly Father is perfect." And besides the command to be "perfect," we find it is not so ridiculous to use God as our model for behavior. In Matthew, Jesus commands us to be like the Father.

We must develop into those people of God who respect others without any thought for ourselves. So often, we excuse ourselves, saying the other people must respect us first, but that is a very earthly, very egocentric view. It is certainly not the clear teaching of Scripture.

Many have received salvation by God's grace through His Son Jesus Christ. But what they have received by God's grace, they must now become in their experience. And this requires personal effort. God never claimed the "working out" process of our salvation was to be a simple one. That process is to be accomplished with "fear and trembling" (Phil 2:12).

Be Forgiving of Sin

Two scriptural characters consistently offer forgiveness to those who sin against them; the first of these is God, and the second is the incarnation of God, Jesus Christ. Looking briefly at the paralleled manner in which both old and new testaments begin provides ample illustration concerning this.

In the book of Genesis, many things occur, but the one most predominate event is the creation of the world. On the sixth day, the creative process climaxes when God brings man and woman into existence. As the Bible then moves into the book of Exodus, it is clear that God's crowning achievement, man and woman, are in need of deliverance from their bondage. In a very real sense, God "re-creates" His people in that they become liberated but also emerge as a brand new people of God. God takes them from the house of bondage and leads them into the Land of Promise.

It must be pointed out that God offers His deliverance before requiring any commitment by the people. It is only after the Israelites are safely removed from Pharaoh's grasp that the people of Israel are given opportunity to accept the covenant relationship proposed by God in Exodus 19.

In the book of Matthew, we again find creation. This time, of course, it is the Saviour, Jesus Christ who is born of God. The apostle Paul refers to Him as the "firstborn of all creation" (Col 1:15).

Jesus arrives on the scene primarily because the people of God are, once again, in bondage. The people are in need of liberation from a political ruler, as they were in the book of Exodus, but the greater focus of Christ's energies are directed at the spiritual portion of the people's bondage.

As God desired to give the children of Israel an opportunity to serve and worship Him primarily through the work of Moses, so did God work through Jesus Christ that a bridge might be formed between Himself and an unholy people. Again, it must be pointed out that deliverance is offered before any commitment or acceptance is in place. Jesus Christ did not require a response from His people before He made the decision to provide opportunity for the removal of their sin.

On the contrary, Jesus Christ made provision for removal of sin from every person; and all this without any expectation of return. As a result, deliverance waits for any person who is willing to accept what has already been solidified on the cross.

As these paralleled testamental "beginnings" are examined, the willingness of God to forgive His people shines forth with tremendous clarity. The people's sojourn in the wilderness and subsequent placement in the Promised Land provides sufficient testimony concerning God's forgiveness. Any person remotely familiar with the Bible knows of the Israelites' repeated complaints and rebellions, their lack of faith and, at times, complete irreverence toward God. And it did not take long for this pattern to emerge.

After ten incredible miracles secured the release of the people, they were almost immediately ready to forfeit their deliverance, invalidate all of God's work, and return to their slavery. At the banks of the Red Sea, with Pharaoh and his army approaching,

> [T]he people of Israel cried out to the LORD; and they said to Moses, "Is it because there are no graves in Egypt that you have taken us away to die in the wilderness? What have you done to us, in bringing us out of Egypt? Is not this what we said to you in Egypt, `Let us alone and let us serve the Egyptians'? For it would have been better for us to serve the Egyptians than to die in the wilderness" (Exod 14:10-12).

As it did not take long for Adam and Eve to be disobedient, neither did it take the Israelites much time to demonstrate their inability and/or their unwillingness to place their trust in God and position their allegiance with Him. And as similar incidents of dissatisfaction and resistance occur through the wilderness wanderings, the only thing more striking than the people's stubbornness is God's capacity to forgive and bring the people a step closer to the Land of Promise.

If demonstration of God's forgiveness and grace under the old covenant are not enough, we find God continuing to "re-create" His people under the new covenant. Through an examination of the person and work of Jesus Christ, we cannot help but be even more impressed with God's love and the lengths to which He is willing to go that His people might always receive one more opportunity to enter into a relationship with Him.

The people of our world are not all that different from the people of Israel. In fact, the book of Exodus should be read as though it is a mirror into our own hearts and dispositions. Like the Israelites, the people of our world do not readily accept a position of subservience and reliance upon the Lord. And as the Israelites continually found new ways to distance themselves from Moses and Aaron, so do the people of our day find new ways to distance themselves from one another.

Seemingly at every turn, people find ways to strain their associations with one another. One person is ridiculed and belittled, another is unaccepted, and yet another is ostracized and abandoned. People are ill-equipped to establish and sustain a relationship; they are much more adept at creating tension in relationships, even severing them completely.

And when it comes to forgiveness, there are some who seemingly lack the capacity altogether. Generally speaking, people choose instead to highlight sin and to lift it up for others to see. Like the accusers of the adulterous woman in John 8, many are compelled to make a public spectacle of sin, obviously believing they themselves lack any shortcoming.

These same self-righteous people often times brand sinners as being such indefinitely, treating them as though they have somehow excluded themselves from all further graces of God. This "branding" occurs primarily with those who have come into salvation but have "backslidden." Ironically, the same does not hold true for the person entrenched in sin prior to salvation. This person's sinful past is, at times, displayed like a trophy.

If a youth pastor, for example, was a man well familar with sin prior to his conversion, it then becomes acceptable for him to make mention of his former debaucheries. It is as though the testimony regarding his sins serve to give him, his salvation and his ministry a certain credibility.

Where does the Bible say the person who accepts Jesus Christ must immediately cease from all sinful activity, never to stumble in any way again lest he be forever consigned to the fires of hell?

> For I know that nothing good dwells within me, that is, in my flesh. I can will what is right, but I cannot do it. For I do not do the good I want, but the evil I do not want is what I do. Now if I do what I do not want, it is no longer I that do it, but sin which dwells within me (Rom 7:18-20).

> My brethren, if any one among you wanders from the truth and some one brings him back, let him know that whoever brings back a sinner from the error of his way will save his soul from death and will cover a multitude of sins (James 5:19-20).

And from our discussion of Jesus washing his disciples' feet in John 13, we are reminded that, symbolically, Jesus was acting out his death on the cross. Therefore, as Jesus knelt before Judas, Judas was being forgiven of his betrayal. Clearly, Judas "knew better" than to betray the Son of God, but Jesus offered him the benefits of His soon-coming work on the cross of Calvary. Even for Judas, the cross of Jesus Christ was effective unto the forgiveness of sin.

Now, let there be no mistake that the Scriptures in no way grant a person license to sin. Just because God is one who repeatedly forgives a sinful offender does not mean a person can willingly and knowingly sin, and expect to receive God's forgiveness. Quite the contrary.

> What shall we say then? Are we to continue in sin that grace may abound? By no means! How can we who died to sin still live in it? Do you not know that all of us who have been baptized into Christ Jesus were baptized into his death? We were buried therefore with him by baptism into death, so that as Christ was raised from the dead by the glory of the Father, we too might walk in newness of life (Rom 6:1-4).

The Bible makes it clear that a person born of Christ is not to walk in his former ways. And if that former way is forgotten by the grace of God, it seems logical to assume it should not be lauded by God's people either, no matter what the motivation.

But Scriptures speak of "willful sinning" in even stronger terms such as in the epistle to the Hebrews. Here, we must remember that the author is making reference to those who sin with no regard for the salvation offered them, pursuing a course that is both spiteful and prideful. But the consequences of such attitudes are worthy of notation.

> For if we sin deliberately after receiving the knowledge of the truth, there no longer remains a sacrifice for sins, but a fearful prospect of judgment, and a fury of fire which will consume the

adversaries. A man who has violated the law of Moses dies without mercy at the testimony of two or three witnesses. How much worse punishment do you think will be deserved by the man who has spurned the Son of God, and profaned the blood of the covenant by which he was sanctified, and outraged the Spirit of grace? (Heb 10:26-29).

It is good to remember that such punishment exists for those who mock and defy the blood of Jesus Christ, but for those of us who have received salvation, our task is not to denounce but to liberate, not to criticize but to deliver, not to condemn, but to forgive.

Then Peter came up and said to him, "Lord, how often shall my brother sin against me, and I forgive him? As many as seven times?" Jesus said to him, "I do not say to you seven times, but seventy times seven (Matt 18:21-22).

But if any one has caused pain, he has caused it not to me, but in some measure--not to put it too severely--to you all. For such a one this punishment by the majority is enough; so you should rather turn to forgive and comfort him, or he may be overwhelmed by excessive sorrow. So I beg you to reaffirm your love for him (2 Cor 2:5-8).

For if you forgive men their trespasses, your heavenly Father also will forgive you; but if you do not forgive men their trespasses, neither will your Father forgive your trespasses (Matt 6:14-15).

We are to be in the business of doing what Jesus Christ did on the cross of Calvary, forgiving people of their sins. We are not to highlight sin, but to cover it. This we do by our words, our thoughts, and our actions. Never must we be responsible for placing another person in bondage, for we are truly doing as Christ would have us when we are delivering people. And this, as we shall see in the next section, can be accomplished in a variety of ways.

Be a Deliverer

The Scriptures teach in various ways and portions that those who are followers of the Lord are expected to continue the work established by the Lord. Perhaps no clearer demonstration exists than in the book of Acts, with the story of Stephen.

Often, what is found beneath the spoken layer of Scripture speaks the more profound and meaningful message communicated by the biblical writer. This is certainly the case with the story of Stephen; while the superficial layer teaches of an obedient man of God willing to die for his faith, the deeper, more poignant layer instructs all disciples to characterize and exemplify, even go so far as to embody the person, work, quality and character of the Lord Jesus Christ.

This can be illustrated by pointing out the striking and deliberate parallels between the story of Stephen and the person and experiences of Jesus: (1) Stephen performed great signs and wonders (Acts 6:8), (2) Stephen was brought before the Council and false witnesses spoke against him (Acts 6:13), (3) Stephen's face shone like the face of an angel (Acts 6:15) as did Jesus' at the mount of transfiguration (Matt 17:2), (4) Stephen saw the heavens opened (Acts 7:56) as did Jesus at His baptism (Matt 3:16), (5) Stephen cried, "Lord Jesus, receive my spirit" (Acts 7:59), (6) Stephen said of those stoning him, "Lord, do not hold this sin against them" (Acts 7:60), and (7) Stephen was put to death (Acts 7:60).

The comparisons are too numerous and conspicuous to be coincidental. Clearly, Stephen has assumed the role of Jesus Christ, in effect, taking the place of Jesus in His absence. And incidentally, Luke also makes it clear Jesus assumed a new role Himself, having taken His place at God's side; when Stephen sees the heavens opened, he sees Jesus standing at the right hand of God (Acts 7:55). Simply said, Stephen has taken Jesus' place on earth while Jesus has assumed the role of the Father in heaven.

The message found in the story of Stephen is that Jesus' followers are to embody the work and person of Jesus in His absence. The work of the Lord is to be carried on and that work, more than anything else, involved the deliverance and/or salvation of the people of God.

Concerning the deliverance of people, there is a predominate understanding of its nature that is far too restrictive; there is a tendency to believe that delivering a person involves only spiritual renewal or regeneration. But deliverance entails much more than leading a person through the sinner's prayer.

Two things must be remembered: (1) the majority of Jesus' miracles and works were not directly related to the spiritual regeneration of a person or persons, and (2) meeting needs which are not related directly to the spirit still have value that is decidedly spiritual. In other words, people's needs encompass many different areas and spiritual benefits can be received from very "terrestrial" acts.

According to the biblical record, there is no question that Jesus healed many physical infirmities. Any person familiar with the gospel literature requires no persuasion here. Jesus not only healed a great variety of physical illnesses and maladies, but a great number of them as well.

And when Jesus entered Peter's house, he saw his mother-in-law lying sick with a fever; he touched her hand, and the fever left her, and she rose and served him. That evening they brought to him many who were possessed with demons, and he cast out the spirits with a word, and healed all who were sick. This was to fulfil what was spoken by the prophet Isaiah, "He took our infirmities and bore our diseases" (Matt 8:14-17).

Jesus spent much time healing the physical infirmities of the people, but naturally, He was also concerned about their spiritual well-being. After all, His entire ministry would culminate in one magnificent act that would have world-wide spiritual significance. Considering how Jesus' followers saw one physical healing after another, it is not surprising they, at times, lost sight of what must be considered to be Jesus' more centralized reason for being.

After a time when the disciples saw Jesus confronted by an unusually large number of people possessing various illnesses and handicaps, there was a paralytic brought before Jesus. It was at this time that Jesus said something very strange, for after seeing the man's faith, Jesus said, "Take heart, my son; your sins are forgiven" (Matt 9:2). Certainly, the disciples must have thought these words unusual for at least two reasons: (1) the man was obviously brought to Jesus that his paralysis might be healed, and (2) only God could forgive sins. The disciples were not the only ones who thought these words of Jesus very strange. "And behold, some of the scribes said to themselves, "This man is blaspheming" (Matt 9:3).

Jesus had healed hundreds, likely thousands of people. And one resulting problem from these extraordinary acts was that He was becoming known as a healer. This was a classification that was clouding His full nature. Jesus Christ was not one of many healers who occupied the land; His position was of much greater distinction and significance than this. And when the paralyzed man was brought forward, Jesus took this opportunity to impress upon the people the extent of His true capacity.

> But Jesus, knowing their thoughts, said, "Why do you think evil in your hearts? For which is easier, to say, `Your sins are forgiven,' or to say, `Rise and walk'? But that you may know that the Son of man has authority on earth to forgive sins"--he then said to the paralytic-- "Rise, take up your bed and go home." And he rose and went home (Matt 9:4-7).

Jesus did not "prove" His supernatural position for prideful reasons; the people absolutely needed to know Jesus Christ could directly meet their spiritual needs. Jesus understood the importance of the people looking to Him for such benefit, not only while He walked among them, but more importantly, after He died on the cross.

As Jesus walked this earth, meeting the various physical needs of the people, so must we adopt the same procedure. As various needs are brought to our attention, we must meet those needs as best we can. Perhaps we are unable to instantly heal physical maladies, but there are an endless number of ways to relieve physical hardship.

As we saw in James, there is great importance in feeding and clothing those less fortunate (James 2:15-16). James also instructs the people of faith to ease emotional hardship, giving as examples the importance of visiting the orphans and the widows (James 1:27).

People sometimes forget that ministering to people's physical and emotional needs is part of Christian responsibility. But what they also forget is that these ministries have a direct bearing on spiritual health as well. All are connected, and therefore, all benefit when only one is nurtured. When one area finds consolation, the others benefit as well.

This is not to say that spiritual regeneration is accomplished through physical and emotional health and well-being. Naturally, it is not. But, at the same time, a person's spiritual well-being is directly affected when that person is ministered to on an emotional and/or physical level. Jesus knew this, and as He practiced these ministries, so must we.

> Then the King will say to those at his right hand, `Come, O blessed of my Father, inherit the kingdom prepared for you from the foundation of the world; for I was hungry and you gave me food, I was thirsty and you gave me drink, I was a stranger and you welcomed me, I was naked and you clothed me, I was sick and you visited me, I was in prison and you came to me.' Then the righteous will answer him, `Lord, when did we see thee hungry and feed thee, or thirsty and give thee drink? And when did we see thee sick or in prison and visit thee? And the King will answer them, `Truly, I say to you, as you did it to one of the least of these my brethren, you did it to me'" (Matt 25:34-40).

Jesus came to earth primarily to meet the spiritual needs of His people, to give them opportunity to be reconciled to the Father. But, unquestionably, Jesus had concern for other aspects of His people's lives as well. As we have seen, He was interested in their physical well-being and their emotional health. But He also demonstrated consideration for their sense of dignity and self-respect.

On more than one occasion, Jesus disregarded cultural and societal norms in order to fulfill His higher calling of ministering to the people. For example, when He spent time with the woman of Samaria in John 4, he was breaching at least two established rules of societal protocol: (1) He was teaching a woman in public, and (2) He was speaking to a Samaritan, a person of mixed Gentile blood. For a Jew, especially one who was a teacher, speaking to either a woman or a Samaritan, was a violation of propriety. Yet Jesus did both, and without regard for appearance or popularity.

As Jesus demonstrated on many occasions, He was much more interested in ministering to people than He was societal convention. Through the story in John 4, it is clear the Samaritan woman was in great need of spiritual enlightenment. And Jesus instructed her. It was very good Jesus overlooked cultural biases and prejudices, for that conversation with the Samaritan woman sparked a city-wide revival.

> Many Samaritans from that city believed in him because of the woman's testimony, "He told me all that I ever did." So when the Samaritans came to him, they asked him to stay with them; and he stayed there two days. And many more believed because of his word. They said to the woman, "It is no longer because of your words that we believe, for we have heard for ourselves, and we know that this is indeed the Savior of the world" (John 4:39-42).

In this story, Jesus demonstrated more than a concern for the spiritual well-being of the people of this world. He displayed a genuine desire to remove obstacles and hindrances; community solidarity had broken down and Jesus worked to restore it. And Jesus did not simply teach the importance of these issues; He stepped forward and took action Himself.

Additionally, human dignity and self-respect were at stake. The Samaritans were treated by the Jews as though they were less than human. Jesus knew that if He put forth effort to reinstate basic human values such as these, the spiritual life would be touched as well. Jesus was compelled to act for several reasons, and the result was city-wide revival.

Jesus' actions are often times interpreted in terms far too monochromatic. Jesus' actions are filled with more meaning than the surface structure would indicate. For example, when Jesus healed a leper, He surely had in mind accomplishing more than the physical healing of that affliction; so much more was involved.

Lepers were shunned by society, excluded from community activities. Considered to be both physically and spiritually unclean, their presence not only raised questions, but brought discomfort. By law, they were forced to bring indignity upon themselves, having to cry out "unclean! unclean!" whenever someone approached.

That lepers could not participate in community activities was understandable to Jesus, but it was also unacceptable.

> When he came down from the mountain, great crowds followed him, and behold, a leper came to him and knelt before him, saying, "Lord, if you will, you can make me clean." And he stretched out his hand and touched him, saying, "I will; be clean." And immediately his leprosy was cleansed (Matt 8:1-3).

Jesus' concerns for people took Him beyond spiritual instruction and physical restoration. In the case of lepers, there was a need for physical healing, but perhaps there was a greater need for their self-respect to be restored, their self-esteem to be rejuvenated and their community participation to be reestablished.

Jesus Christ came into the world to deliver people, but deliverance encompasses a much broader scope than that perceived by those who see salvation as that which reconciles the sinner to the

Father. And as Jesus Christ's followers have taken on Jesus' role in this world, they must be involved in more than direct spiritual instruction concerning reconciliation.

"Delivering" people involves many different, if not an infinite number of areas. Christ's followers must be willing to forgive and to reconcile, but they must also attend to physical and emotional needs; they must put forth energy to offer encouragement, provide comfort, restore confidence, motivate the discouraged, and on and on the list goes.

As we saw in chapter two, followers of Jesus Christ are expected to be the salt and the light of the earth (Matt 5:13-14). Salt is essentially different from the substance into which it is placed. Like salt, Christians must act as moral disinfectants, preserving morality and arresting decay.

As light, Christians reveal all that is known about God, illuminating people as to who God is. As we have seen, this involves an entire arena of thoughts, attitudes and actions; it is accomplished, not so much by words, but by actions.

> You are the salt of the earth; but if salt has lost its taste, how shall its saltness be restored? It is no longer good for anything except to be thrown out and trodden under foot by men. You are the light of the world. A city set on a hill cannot be hid. Nor do men light a lamp and put it under a bushel, but on a stand, and it gives light to all in the house. Let your light so shine before men, that they may see your good works and give glory to your Father who is in heaven (Matt 5:13-16).

Be Always Positive

At times, Satan is accomplishing what he hopes to in the lives of the people of this world; contentious spirits predominate, discord is spread and disharmony prevails. This is always distressing. But, what is even more disturbing is when Satan's works are accomplished without his activity, when so-called "Christians" are accomplishing these things without his direct influence.

Satan does not need to prowl about like a roaring lion when the supposed lambs are successfully attacking the church from its most vulnerable point: the inside. What does this say about the church when quarreling and division are regular occurrences? What impression is left in the minds of those who see the church divided by factions, weakened by ongoing disputes?

This is exactly one of the points the apostle Paul was making in his first letter to the Corinthians when he instructed believers to settle disputes among themselves. They were instructed in this manner, not solely because conflicts disrupt harmony within the church but because this kind of activity sends the worst kind of message to those outside the church.

When one of you has a grievance against a brother, does he dare go to law before the unrighteous instead of the saints? Do you not know that the saints will judge the world? And if the world is to be judged by you, are you incompetent to try trivial cases? Do you not know that we are to judge angels? How much more, matters pertaining to this life! If then you have such cases, why do you lay them before those who are least esteemed by the church? I say this to your shame. Can it be that there is no man among you wise enough to decide between members of the brotherhood, but brother goes to law against brother, and that before unbelievers? (1 Cor 6:1-6)

In a very real sense, the church is failing in its efforts to transform the world. Whereas God expects His people to recast, even revolutionize the ungodly superstructure of this world, the church has succeeded, to a large degree, in becoming conformed to the world, adopting the world's various attitudes, dispositions and demeanors. The church is, very simply, not the transforming force God expects.

> I appeal to you therefore, brethren, by the mercies of God, to present your bodies as a living sacrifice, holy and acceptable to God, which is your spiritual worship. Do not be conformed to this world but be transformed by the renewal of your mind, that you may prove what is the will of God, what is good and acceptable and perfect (Rom 12:1-2).

What is "good and acceptable and perfect" can never involve attitudes and perspectives finding expression through biting sarcasm, antagonistic criticism, and slanderous accusation. These and expressions like them are all too commonplace, perhaps not so much within the various church buildings, but certainly among many so-called "Christians."

As we have seen previously, the tongue projects what the heart feels; it sends a message that runs parallel to what a person thinks and believes. And in far too many cases, the tongue of a believer reveals a heart lacking confidence and faith, a heart that is anything but certain of God and God's people. All too often, precisely the opposite message is conveyed.

How can a person who is consistently negative about nearly every person and every thing be considered to have a proper amount of faith in God? Name a topic of discussion in that person's presence and the forthcoming comments are regularly pessimistic, at times fatalistic. It does not matter if the subject is the weather or another body of believers or the name of a person mutually known. The comments are everything but positive.

Satan enjoys great advances in the body of believers, and this, often times, by no effort of his own. Far too many believers look around and see everything as mishandled, mismanaged, needing improvement, or riddled with error. For these believers, all of the frailties and weaknesses of humanity are in plain view and to make matters worse, these shortcomings are then dramatized and publicized. This attitude and behavior results in nothing good.

Believers often expend energy to hinder, rather than prosper the kingdom of God. And unfortunately, the negative attitudes and language spawn even more negativity. The snowball effect is such that an entire body of believers can become infected. And, often times, as a result, the body of believers become immune to a true perception of how truly ungodly their behavior really is; it is possible for an entire church to become desensitized to their inappropriate behavior.

Do you not know that a little leaven leavens the whole lump? Cleanse out the old leaven that you may be a new lump, as you really are unleavened. For Christ, our paschal lamb, has been sacrificed. Let us, therefore, celebrate the festival, not with the old leaven, the leaven of malice and evil, but with the unleavened bread of sincerity and truth (1 Cor 5:6-8).

Negativity, doubt and pessimism can contaminate an entire body of believers. However, it is important to remember that optimism, enthusiasm and hopefulness are able to restore the morale, even the very faith of the same group. But, it cannot start with the other person, it must begin with us. And when this confidence is found, it must not waver; regardless of the opposition, the optimism must remain a constant, never allowing itself to be disappointed, disheartened or discouraged.

If the tongue manifests what the heart feels, it stands to reason that the tongue is also an indicator of how the world is perceived, processed and interpreted. It is an interesting phenomenon that two people's perceptions of the same thing can be vastly different. Where one person sees potential, another sees limitation; where one sees opportunity, another sees futility; where one remains confident, another loses hope.

The Scriptures speak of people with extraordinary faith, even during the most trying, seemingly hopeless situations. For example, Elisha remained absolutely calm even though the entire Syrian army was encamped around the city in which he was staying.

Elisha's servant was with him at the city of Dothan and both knew the Syrian army had come to kill them. Interestingly enough, Elisha's reaction ran counter to his servant's reaction.

When the servant of the man of God rose early in the morning and went out, behold, an army with horses and chariots was round about the city. And the servant said, "Alas, my master! What shall we do?" He said, "Fear not, for those who are with us are more than those who are with them" (2 Kgs 6:15-16).

And of course, Elisha was right. After the prophet prayed for his servant's eyes to be opened, the servant looked to the hills and saw them filled with horses and chariots of fire (2 Kgs 6:17).

Before the Red Sea, the Israelites and Moses both saw Pharaoh's army approaching, but again, the responses were anything but similar.

> When Pharaoh drew near, the people of Israel lifted up their eyes, and behold, the Egyptians were marching after them; and they were in great fear. And the people of Israel cried out to the LORD; and they said to Moses, "Is it because there are no graves in Egypt that you have taken us away to die in the wilderness? What have you done to us, in bringing us out of Egypt? Is not this what we said to you in Egypt, `Let us alone and let us serve the Egyptians'? For it would have been better for us to serve the Egyptians than to die in the wilderness." And Moses said to the people, "Fear not, stand firm, and see the salvation of the LORD, which he will work for you today; for the Egyptians whom you see today, you shall never see again. The LORD will fight for you, and you have only to be still" (Exod 14:10-14).

The Israelites were convinced they were to be slaughtered while Moses maintained a calm assurance concerning the situation. And the same observation can be made about the people of God in our day. Experiencing the same situation, one person will see tremendous victory while the other sees catastrophic defeat; the same world is perceived by different people, but with completely different translations.

Obviously, a person's relationship with God is an important, if not decisive factor. There is much to be said about cultivating a positive attitude within oneself, but when it comes to being faith-filled, there is no substitute for developing a relationship with God that allows nothing to discourage efforts, dampen attitudes or discourage spirits.

A close relationship with God gives a person the ability to view things from God's perspective. This assists greatly, for with God, the impossibilities of humanity are commonplace; those things perceived to be supernatural are ordinary and familiar.

Be a Servant's Servant

If a person's duty to God is to be summarized with a four-word command, the words comprising this section's title would work very well, "Be a servant's servant." These words not only remind us we are responsible to, and belong to the greatest servant who ever walked this earth, Jesus Christ, but they also instruct us concerning what is to comprise the very heart of our existence: servitude.

Throughout these previous chapters, it has been maintained that serving God is accomplished only by serving God's people. Jeremiah taught us in chapter one that God's people must bear fruit with their lives, but that this is accomplished only by much perseverance. In the same chapter, we learned from Moses' example that God's people are not necessarily born servants, but fashioned and molded into servants by and through experience, as interaction occurs with both God and people.

Servitude begins inside a person, with the person's heart and soul and spirit. It is not something "practiced" and contrived, but that which rises from a heart of sincerity and a soul filled with truth. Chapter two instructed us of the various ungodly attitudes and responses and expressions which must be either transformed or eliminated. A true servant of God must not be filled with a tendency to express the old nature; the old nature must become brand new.

Chapter three spoke of hypocrisy, how a believer's inner self must be in balance with outer expressions. Love is something that must thoroughly encompass the heart of a follower of Jesus Christ and Paul's first letter to the Corinthians served to remind us of what love really is. Once genuine love is part and parcel of the immaterial portion of ourselves, then this love will naturally flow to the world existing outside ourselves.

Chapter four spoke of Jesus, the true servant, as His person and character were, among other ways, beautifully depicted in the Christ hymn recorded in Philippians 2. As we saw, the description of Jesus is to be adopted into our own lives. And Jesus was nothing if not a servant.

> Have this mind among yourselves, which you have in Christ Jesus, who, though he was in the form of God, did not count equality with God a thing to be grasped, but emptied himself, taking the form of a servant (Phil 2:5-7).

Basically, the need for God's people to become servants is what this book's message has been. Jesus came not to be served, therefore, His people are not to be served, but to serve. And the great variety of ways this is accomplished has been discussed at some length.

It is not easy to humble oneself before all other people, to allow ridicule when none is deserved and to accept punishment when no crime was committed. But perhaps the greatest lesson to be learned from Jesus Christ comes from His willingness to be considered a criminal when He was nothing of the kind; as a direct result of the false accusations against Him and His willingness to be unjustly punished, hundreds of millions of people have had and continue to have opportunity to establish a relationship with God, and one day, see heaven's doors open.

A person cannot be a servant if that person is consumed by pride. Conceit and arrogance make a person unwilling to concede a position and incapable of admitting failure. And with conceit and arrogance being the breeding ground for conflict and controversy, the person struggling with these cannot possibly relate to people in a way

Jesus Christ would have him.

Often, there is much benefit in simply conceding an argument or admitting error. "It was my fault" or "I was wrong" are words that carry tremendous healing power. It is a shame that so many people cannot bring themselves to say them. Instead, people insist on being "right," regardless of the cost, because their own egos carry more importance than does their concern for the feelings of others and the relationships shared. It is not always the best thing to be right; at times, it can be most destructive.

Solitude threatens and placates
Whispering sorrows repeat
Life's softened shadows bring comfort
Demons and angels now meet

Pathways rise up with their greeting
Scorn blankets truth with its dread
Light filters through to the vanquished
Hopefulness rises instead

Various streams reach their limit
Hard-driven crests are at ease
Doves extend sleep with their virtues
Ravens now circle the seas

Warmth plays a song of rare beauty
Disquieted souls cease their moans
Grays are enveloped by scarlet
Depths harbor faint distant tones

P. L. Engstrom

Conclusion

There are basically two kinds of people in this world, those living at the top of the mountain with Moses and those engaged in self-willed, self-engrossed egocentrism at the bottom. When Moses was at the top, he was removed from the self-destructive practices and also in the presence of God. But more than this, he was pleading with God not to destroy the people for their sins. This is a most beautiful picture of a person who has transcended an earthly existence with all of its trappings; in a single image, we see that Moses (1) had escaped ungodliness, (2) found the Lord and was in His presence, and (3) was interceding on behalf of the people, offering his own life in exchange for theirs.

At the bottom of the mountain, the people's activity testified of their distance from God. They were self-gratifying, absorbed with their own desires and needs. They were not servants at all, but people so disgusting to God, He was determined to destroy them.

We must ask ourselves some questions: Where are our loyalties? Are we far from God, cocooned within ourselves and our worlds, looking to gratify yet another desire or whim? Or, are we with Moses at the top of the mountain? Have we transcended the pettiness and the arrogance and the corruption? Or are we looking for new ways to be served that our weak egos might be fed? Are we placing the well-being of others before our own? Or are we still self-indulgent, waiting continuously for others to please us?

Answering these questions should provide a person with the ability to answer some questions everyone asks about eternity. Where will we spend it? What exactly awaits us on the other side? Will heaven's doors be opened or will they be closed?

God has provided us with every opportunity to answer these questions in a way that is most positive, because He has already decided where He would like us to spend eternity. Through His Son, Jesus Christ, we have received God's most gracious act. But now comes the hard part--putting into practice what we have already received by God's grace. Are we willing to do what is necessary? The decision lies with us.